The Catholic
Theological Union
LIBRARY
Chicago, Ill.
WITHDRAWN

Gods, Priests, and Warriors

The Bhṛgus of the *Mahābhārata*

Studies in Oriental Culture, Number 12
Columbia University

Gods, Priests, and Warriors

The Bhṛgus of the *Mahābhārata*

Robert P. Goldman

New York · Columbia University Press · 1977

The Andrew W. Mellon Foundation, through a special grant,
has assisted the Press in publishing this volume.

Columbia University Press
New York Guildford, Surrey

Library of Congress Cataloging in Publication Data

Goldman, Robert P 1942–
Gods, priests, and warriors.

(Studies in Oriental Culture)
Bibliography: p.
Includes index.
1. Bhṛgus. 2. Mahābhārata. I. Title.
II. Series.
BL1132.B49G64 294.5′923 76–41255
ISBN: 0–231–03941–7

Studies in Oriental Culture
Edited at Columbia University

Acknowledgments

The present work owes its existence to the inspiration and assistance of many of my teachers, colleagues, and friends. Some, however, were, I fear, put to special pains on my behalf. My teachers Drs. Ernest Bender and Ludo Rocher of the University of Pennsylvania offered many valuable suggestions. Dr. Barbara Miller of Barnard College read through a massive and complex early draft and suggested numerous ways in which it could be simplified. My friend Dr. J. M. Masson of the University of Toronto was a constant source of advice and encouragement during the years that we worked together in India. His scholarship and generosity are as much as any other factor responsible for the completion of the work. My thanks also to Paṇḍit Dr. V. W. Paranjpe, Paṇḍit Ramaṇācarya, and Paṇḍit Śrīnivāsa Śāstrī of the Deccan College for their help in the elucidation of many textual difficulties.

I am especially grateful to the American Institute of Indian Studies and the Committee on Research of the University of California at Berkeley for the support required for the conduct of the research represented here and for the production of the manuscript.

Mr. Douglas Walker read through the first draft and assisted with numerous editorial problems. Special thanks are also due to Ms. Sally Sutherland, and Mr. Denis Lahey, without whose patience and dedication my notes might even now be lying heaped around my desk.

ROBERT P. GOLDMAN

Contents

Abbreviations

A	Aurva
ABORI	*Annals of the Bhandarkar Oriental Research Institute*
ABr	*Aitareya Brāhmaṇa*
Ādi	Ādiparvan
AgniP	*Agnipurāṇa*
AJP	*American Journal of Philology*
Anus	Anuśāsanaparvan
Āraṇyaka	Āraṇyakaparvan
ASS	Ānandāśrama Sanskrit Series
AV	*Atharvaveda*
BhG	*Bhagavadgītā*
BhP	*Bhāgavatapurāṇa*
BrahmaP	*Brahmapurāṇa*
BrahmāṇḍP	*Brahmāṇḍapurāṇa*
C	Cyavana
CK	Cyavana and Kuśika
Citr. ed.	Citraśālā Press edition of the *Mbh*
Crit. ed.	Critical edition of the *Mbh*, V. S. Sukthankar, et al., eds.
HV	*Harivaṃśa*

IHQ	*Indian Historical Quarterly*
JAOS	*Journal of the American Oriental Society*
JBr	*Jaiminīya Brāhmaṇa*
JIH	*Journal of Indian History*
JOIB	*Journal of the Oriental Institute of Baroda*
JRAS	*Journal of the Royal Asiatic Society*
JUB	*Journal of the University of Bombay*
JUN	*Journal of the University of Nagpur*
KSS	*Kathāsaritsāgara*
MatsyaP	*Matsyapurāṇa*
Mbh	*Mahābhārata*
Manu	*Manusmṛti*
MS	*Maitrāyaṇī Saṃhitā*
Nīl.	Nīlakaṇṭha
PadmaP	*Padmapurāṇa*
PBr	*Pañcaviṃśa Brāhmaṇa*
PCK	*Prācīnacaritrakośa*
R	Rāma
Rām	*Rāmāyaṇa*
RV	*Ṛgveda*
ŚA	Śukra and the Asuras
Śānti	Śāntiparvan
ŚBr	*Śatapatha Brāhmaṇa*
SK	Śukra and Kaca
SkP	*Skandapurāṇa*
ŚŚ	Śukra and Śiva
TA	*Taittirīya Āraṇyaka*
TBr	*Taittirīya Brāhmaṇa*
TS	*Taittirīya Saṃhitā*
TU	*Taittirīya Upaniṣad*
UK	Uttarakāṇḍa

VāmanaP	*Vāmanapurāṇa*
VāyuP	*Vāyupurāṇa*
ViṣP	*Viṣṇupurāṇa*
ZDMG	*Zeitschrift der Deutschen Morgenländischen Gesellschaft*

Introduction

In the course of his extensive critical study of India's great epic, the *Mahābhārata*, V. S. Sukthankar observed a phenomenon the significance of which had hitherto escaped the attention of scholars.[1] He noticed that a disproportionate amount of the mythic and legendary material with which the text abounds is given over to the histories and exploits of the representatives of one priestly clan, the Bhṛgus or Bhārgavas.

> Taking a collective view of the Bhārgava references in the Great Epic, we cannot avoid the conclusion that the Bhārgava heroes occupy a surprisingly large portion of the canvas—which is said to depict the Bhārata War—filling up as they do much of the available space of the background. And it is more than probable that if the epic is examined yet more minutely, still further evidence of Bhārgava material, hitherto undiscovered, will be brought to light. The figures of the Bhārgavas have also been magnified to colossal proportions, painted with a thick brush and in vivid colours. Their myths and legends are uniformly distributed over the entire extent of the Great Epîc with the exception of some short and uninteresting parvans. . . .[2]

A critical although not very elaborate survey of this material convinced Sukthankar that the Bhārgava myths of the epic were distinguished by more than their abundance. He found that these myths tended to exalt the Bhṛgus to a degree striking even for the often hyperbolic *Mahābhārata*, and that, moreover, they frequently appeared at critical junctures in the epic. "There should be, therefore, in my opinion, no hesitation in concluding that in our version of the *Mahābhārata* there is a conscious—nay deliberate—weaving together of the Bhārata legends with the Bhārgava stories."[3] These discoveries led Sukthankar, finally, to posit his famous theory of a thoroughgoing revision of the warrior epic at the hands of Bhārgava redactors.[4] This theory has proven basic to all subsequent study of the *Mahābhārata*.

Nonetheless, Sukthankar's work raised many more questions than it answered. For, having posited his theory of the Bhṛguid recension, he shied away from the problems of the content of the Bhārgava myths, their structure, and their mutual relationship.[5]

These problems, however, are of the utmost significance, especially insofar as their investigation may shed light on the issues of the formation and functions of Indian epic literature. It is to this investigation that the present work is dedicated.

A comprehensive study of the Bhṛgus and Bhārgava mythology is a desideratum. Aside from Sukthankar's essay, the great bulk of scholarly effort in this area has been directed to but one Bhārgava figure, Paraśurāma.[6] The Bhṛgus as a group and the other fascinating Bhārgavas have generally been studied only to the extent that they appear to contribute to this effort. The results of such studies have been disappointing.[7] Major figures such as Cyavana and Uśanas Kāvya (Śukra), who appear throughout the literature in the most provocative mythic contexts, have been largely ignored, as has the significance of the Bhṛgus in the Veda, which would surely well repay scholarly investigation.

A comprehensive study of the Bhṛgus would, however, have to be a long and complex one. The group and its various members appear, in roles of greater or lesser significance, throughout the immense corpus of Indian mythological literature from the earliest Veda to the latest purāṇic texts, turning up even in the popular cults of several areas of the country.[8] The present work will attempt nothing so ambitious. Except where vedic and purāṇic material sheds some special light on the Bhārgava mythology of the *Mahābhārata*, it will be avoided.

There are several reasons for this, aside from the problem of size. Although the Bhṛgus appear in many texts, it is only the *Mahābhārata* that they may be said to dominate. The *Bhārata* is the definitive Bhārgava text. It therefore presents what no other text can show: an extensive and complex Bhārgava submythology that has been deliberately worked into its fabric. Because of this, the Bhārgava corpus of the *Mahābhārata* is to a certain extent consistent, and is a largely self-referent system. In contrast, the Bhārgava myths of other texts, texts over which no pervasive Bhārgava influence can be demonstrated, do not generally occupy so conspicuous a place. Thus the Bhṛgus of the vedic literature are neither insignificant[9] nor especially prominent.

The Purāṇas present, typically, a complicated picture. It is true that certain of the Bhṛgu sages are exalted to even higher status than they are accorded in the epic.[10] On the other hand, most Bhṛguid episodes in the Purāṇas are versions of epic myths inflated for sectarian rather than Bhārgava purposes.[11] In any case, the Bhārgava sages of the purāṇic literature are not, on the whole, accorded the redactors' special fervor that distinguishes them from other groups in the *Mahābhārata*.

The Purāṇas are also to be distinguished from the *Mahābhārata* on textual grounds. Under the guiding spirit of Sukthankar, the great epic has been published in an excellent critical edition.[12] This great work has greatly facilitated the present study by making it immediately clear just which portions of the various myths belong to the best reconstruction of the text and which do not. No such work is as yet available for the great bulk of even the Mahāpurāṇas, and the task of analyzing the structure and interrelations of the purāṇic myths is therefore more uncertain.

It is the *Mahābhārata* alone[13] that presents a Bhārgava context for the myths. By the same token, the nature of the mythogenic process in the Indian epic and the form and function of the *Mahābhārata* itself are uniquely illuminated by the Bhārgava corpus.

The Bhṛgus of the Bhārata: a Race Apart

The Bhṛgus or Bhārgavas as they are known to the epic are a family of brahman seers and priests descended from an eponymous ancestor, the great ṛṣi Bhṛgu.[14] As such they are similar to the priestly descendants of the other great ṛṣis. Bhṛguid myth, however, is somewhat more consistently aware of familial affiliation than myths of the other great sages. Indeed, questions of highly charged family relationships are almost an obsession of the Bhārgava mythmakers.

It is not only their prominence, the proliferation of their myths in the *Mahābhārata*, that sets the Bhṛgus apart from the other brahmanical clans who, with warriors, gods, demons, etc., people the vast poem. The myths themselves are unusual because of the themes and motifs that recur throughout the corpus and, indeed, form its characteristic subepisodic elements. These elements, notable in the individual myths but compelling in the mass, unequivocally mark the Bhṛgus as a group set apart from their fellow brahmans.

The themes that form the heart of the Bhārgava corpus, taken collectively, establish a pattern of behavior that is aberrant with respect to the norms of brahmanical activities set forth in the dharma literature, including the *Mahābhārata* itself. The central concerns of the Bhṛgus appear from the mythology to have included death, violence, sorcery, confusion and violation of class-roles (*varṇāśramadharma*), intermarriage with other varṇas (*varṇasaṃkara*), and open hostility to the gods themselves. In addition, several of the Bhārgava sages are shown in the epic to have engaged with impunity in such activities as theft, drinking liquor, and killing a woman, acts that are condemned unequivocally in the law texts as especially improper for brahmans.[15] One of the greatest of the Bhṛgus is everywhere said to have served as the priest and chaplain of the *asuras*, the demon enemies of heaven and of order (*dharma*).

Themes and Motifs

Some of the themes characteristic of the Bhṛgus are occasionally associated with sages of other families. Indeed, in a number of instances it is apparent that the Bhārgava editors have not scrupled to borrow motifs from non-Bhārgava myths. Yet the fact remains that what is sporadic among the non-Bhārgavas has become systematic among the Bhṛgus. In general, Bhārgava myth of the epic has no major concerns apart from those mentioned; these central themes are repeated time and again in different contexts, in different myths, and in connection with different Bhṛgus.

The internal coherence of the Bhārgava cycle provided the key to the methodology of the present work. The basic procedure was to read closely the Bhārgava mythology of the *Mahābhārata*, to analyze the various versions of the individual myths, and to identify, isolate, and compare their submythic structural elements.[16] These, in turn, were considered, where appropriate, in the contexts of related non-Bhārgava epic myth and Bhārgava myths of the Vedas and the Purāṇas.

The submythic structural elements have been designated "themes" or "motifs." The themes are the basic topical concerns of the Bhṛguid mythmakers, examples being the themes of death and resurrection that dominate the cycle. Frequently these themes express a relation between the Bhṛgus and non-Bhārgava groups. Thus many Bhārgava myths are concerned in whole or in part with the peculiarly ambivalent relations of the Bhṛgus and the *kṣatriyas*, or warrior class. Others deal with the relationship of the clan to the gods and other supernatural beings. Many, in their treatment of Bhārgava participation in unorthodox practices, may be viewed as defining the stance of the Bhṛgus as compared to the other priestly clans of Indian mythology. No theme is confined to only one myth, and few myths are concerned with but one theme.

The motifs are the smaller structural units, specific devices used to elucidate and enliven the central themes. Examples would be the paralysis of a god, the beheading of a woman, the restoration of life to the dead through the use of a specific magical technique. It is characteristic of many of the Bhārgava motifs that they are subject to a process of inversion. Thus the motif of genocide occurs in two forms: in one the Bhṛgus are exterminated by the kṣatriyas, while in the other a Bhṛgu exterminates the warrior class. Again, the Bhārgava Śukra undergoes a special kind of second birth by being ingested and expelled by a god, while in another myth Śukra swallows and later disgorges his pupil, who thereby experiences this same second birth.

Motifs and themes, however inherently interesting, and whatever their origin, were excluded from this study unless they met two tests that qualify them to be regarded as truly Bhārgava. In order to qualify they had to be major elements in at least one Bhārgava myth, and, they had to recur in some form in at least one other Bhārgava myth, preferably in connection with different figures.[17]

The goals of this process of analysis are several and together constitute the purpose of the present work. They are:

1. To isolate and catalog the themes and motifs of the Bhārgava cycle, and to determine as far as possible their original sources and mythic affiliations.

2. To determine whether the recurrent use of submythic structural elements can illuminate the structure of the entire mythic cycle and its relation to other mythic cycles in Sanskrit literature.

3. To provide a basis for assessing the consistently aberrant behavior of the Bhṛgus.

4. To elucidate the function of the cycle in the formation of the *Mahābhārata*.

Myth and Metamyth

Some salient features became evident in the course of the analysis. It became clear that the recurrence of the same structural elements in the various myths must have been intended by the mythic redactors. In fact, some of the most important and widely repeated of the Bhārgava myths that represent the culmination and quintessence of the cycle have been almost wholly created out of these elements. At least one major Bhārgava episode consists largely of an attempt at rationalization of a major subsection of the cycle itself.[18] It is a myth about myth.

These techniques of deliberate, purposeful manipulation of mythic elements are a major characteristic of the cycle and are of the greatest significance to any attempt to understand it. These phenomena can be called metamyth in that they represent mythological material of a decidedly secondary character when compared with the primary material that they restructure and explain. It is clear that a considerable part of the Bhārgava cycle consists of myths about myths[19] and myths composed of the structural elements of other myths. This body of metamythic material provides an unusual opportunity for examining the ways in which the *Mahābhārata*, India's greatest repository of myth and legend, took the form in which we know it.

The proliferation of Bhārgava themes and motifs and the almost baroque complexity of their distribution among the various myths and versions is such that it will be difficult for readers not intimately familiar with the *Mahābhārata* to follow the arguments without some way of being able to refer frequently to the source materials. For this reason I am including as Part 1 of this book translations of the major Bhārgava stories before continuing with the text of the study in Part 2. It is suggested that the reader first read through these translations so that he may be made familiar with the original stories and be thus able to follow the arguments of the text without the need of lengthy and repetitive retellings of the various myths.

Part 1
Bhārgava Myths in Translation

AURVA (= A)
(*Mbh* I.169–71)

Vasiṣṭha said:

(169.11–25) 1. There was a king in the earth called Kṛtavīrya, a great king, for whom the Bhṛgus, knowers of the Vedas, sacrificed in the world.

2. At the end of the soma sacrifice, that lord of the people satisfied them, who were entitled to the first share,[1] with much grain and wealth, my son.

3. Once, when the great king had died, his descendants found themselves in need of money.

4. All the princes, having learned of the wealth of the Bhārgavas, approached the Bhārgava leaders as beggars, my boy.

5. Some of the Bhṛgus realized the danger from the kṣatriyas and hid their vast wealth in the earth, while some gave it to [other] brahmans.

[1] *agrabhuj*: lit. "eating first." The term indicates the precedence accorded to the Bhṛgu priests.

6. Some of the Bhṛgus, perceiving an ulterior motive [?],[2] gave the wealth to the kṣatriyas as they wished.
7. Then a certain kṣatriya who happened to be digging in the earth found the wealth near the house of one of the Bhṛgus. Seeing that wealth, all the kṣatriya lords assembled.
8. In their wrath, these mighty archers disregarded the Bhṛgus who had come to them for refuge, and slew them all with sharp arrows. And so they roamed about the earth killing them, sparing not even the embryos in the womb.
9. Then, when the Bhṛgus were being massacred, the wives of the clan went in fear to the Himavat mountain.
10. One of them, a woman of beautiful thighs, in fear, hid her glorious embryo in one thigh for the perpetuation of her husband's race. They [the kṣatriyas] saw that brahman woman shining with her own glory.[3]
11. Then the embryo split the thigh of the brahman woman and emerged like the midday sun, blinding the kṣatriyas. Deprived of their sight, they wandered about in the dangerous paths of the mountain.

[2] *kāraṇāntaradarśanāt*: lit. "out of perception of another reason." What this means remains unclear to me. The only hidden motive ascribed to the Bhṛgus in this episode is that mentioned at v. 32; there the motive prompts them to hide their wealth. What "other reason" prompts them to give it to the kṣatriyas?

[3] The Citr. ed. inserts six pādas after 10 that read as follows: "A certain brahman woman, learning about the embryo, was overcome with fear, and so she approached the kṣatriyas and told them. Then the kṣatriyas went, prepared to kill the fetus." This has been added, no doubt, to lend greater continuity to the passage. Nīl. explains that the woman was afraid lest the kṣatriyas accuse her of complicity with Aurva's mother.

12. Then the kṣatriya lords, terrified and thwarted in their plans, approached that blameless brahman woman for refuge and for the sake of their sight.
13. The kṣatriyas, distressed, grief stricken, and devoid of luster, like fires whose flames have been extinguished, addressed the great lady:
14. "By your grace, let the kṣatriyas regain their sight. Let us sinners go, as we have given up our plan.
15. May you and your son be gracious to us all. Be pleased to save the princes by restoring their sight."

(170.1–21) 16. The brahman woman said:
"I did not take your sight, my sons, nor am I angry. Rather it is this Bhārgava, born from my thigh, who is furious with you.
17. Surely it is this great being who, remembering his slain kinsmen, has in his wrath taken away your sight.
18. When you, my sons, slew even the embryos of the Bhṛgus, I kept this embryo in my thigh for a hundred years.
19. The entire Veda along with its six subsidiary branches has entered into him, even though he is still an infant, out of a desire once more to assist the race of Bhṛgu.
20. He by whose great brilliance you have been deprived of your sight wishes to destroy you in his anger at the slaying of his ancestors.
21. Entreat this excellent son of mine, Aurva. When he is satisfied with your obeisance, he will restore your sight."
22. The Gandharva said:
When they were addressed in this way, all the princes said "Be appeased!" to Aurva and he was propitiated.

23. Thus was that brahman sage born, after splitting open her thigh. Because of this that great being became known in all the worlds by the name Aurva.[4]
24. When the kings had regained their sight, they returned home. But the Bhārgava sage set his mind on the destruction of the entire world.
25. That great being inclined his thoughts toward the total destruction of all the worlds.
26. Wishing to avenge the Bhṛgus, this great Bhṛgu grew great through great austerities for the destruction of the whole world.
27. With his great and mighty austerities, he heated[5] the worlds, along with their gods, men, and demons, gladdening his ancestors.
28. His ancestors were aware of that, son, and having come from the ancestors' world (*pitṛloka*), spoke this speech to the excellent Bhṛgu [Aurva]:
29. "Aurva, son, we have seen the power of your fierce austerity. Be gracious toward the worlds. Restrain your anger.
30. Son, the contemplative Bhṛgus, who were not helpless, all connived at the murderous kṣatriyas' slaughter.
31. For when weariness with prolonged life came over us, we ourselves desired death at the hands of the kṣatriyas.
32. Indeed, that wealth that someone dug up near the

[4] The name Aurva is here derived from the noun *ūru*, "thigh," and means "born from the thigh."

[5] Austerity is commonly regarded in India as generating heat, which can be destructive. Indeed, the term most often used for austerity, asceticism, and self mortification, *tapas*, is derived from the root *tap* "to heat, grow hot."

dwelling of the Bhṛgus was put there by us, who wanted to anger the kṣatriyas exclusively to provoke hostility. For, great brahman, what use for money have we, who are desirous of heaven?

33. Since by no means is death able to take us, we perceived and agreed upon this device, son.
34. Son, a suicide does not attain auspicious worlds. Considering this, we did not kill ourselves.
35. What you wish to do, son, is not good. Withdraw your mind from sin, from the destruction of the whole world.
36. For neither kṣatriyas nor the seven worlds could vitiate the glory of our austerities. Son, destroy this anger that has arisen."[6]

(171.1–23) Aurva said:

37. "Fathers, the vow to destroy the whole world that I uttered in my anger must not prove false.
38. I cannot live as one whose vow of anger is vain. For this anger, unvented, would burn me up as fire does a fire-stick.
39. A man who suppresses anger that has arisen for a good reason is incapable of protecting the three highest social orders (*trivarga*).
40. Kings desirous of attaining heaven should use anger properly to punish the bad and protect the good.
41. When I was still an embryo, hidden in the thigh, I heard the wailing of the host of the mothers of the Bhṛgus during the kṣatriyas' slaughter.

[6] The Citr. ed. reads: "Do not destroy the kṣatriyas, or the seven worlds, son. Destroy instead that anger that has arisen and is spoiling the power of your austerities." Again, this may be an emendation to make the passage smoother and more continuous.

42. This anger entered me when men and gods tolerated the slaughter of the Bhṛgus, even the embryos in the womb, at the hands of the most wretched kṣatriyas.
43. My mothers, whose wombs were full, and my fathers with full treasuries[7] could find no refuge among men because of fear.
44. At that time no one protected the wives of the Bhṛgus, and the glorious lady bore me in one of her thighs.
45. For when someone to prevent evil is found among the people, no evildoer appears among them.
46. But when a wicked man finds no one at all to restrain him, many in the world engage in evil actions.
47. Moreover, a man—even a ruler—who recognizes evil and, although capable of preventing it, does not is implicated in that evil.
48. The kings and lords did not protect my ancestors, although they were able to do so, for they were thinking only of their own dear lives.
49. Therefore, having now become myself a great lord, I am furious with all the worlds. So I am incapable of carrying out your instructions.
50. Were I, as lord, to neglect the worlds, then there would be great danger because of sin.
51. This anger-born fire of mine that wishes to destroy the worlds would, if held in, consume me by its own brilliance.
52. I know your desire for the welfare of all the worlds. Therefore, lords, prescribe what will be best for the worlds and also for me."

[7] *āpūrṇakośāḥ* should be read punningly. The term *kośa* here means two different things; treasury (in the case of the Bhṛgu fathers) and womb (in the case of the mothers).

53. The ancestors said:
"Cast this fire of yours, born of anger, capable of destroying the worlds, into the waters. For the worlds are founded in the waters.
54. The essence of everything consists of water, as does the whole world. Therefore, great brahman, cast this fire of anger into the waters.
55. If you will, brahman, then let this fire of yours, born from your anger, be placed in the sea to consume the waters. For it is said that the worlds consist of water.
56. Thus, sinless one, will your vow prove true, while men and the gods will not be destroyed."
57. Vasiṣṭha said:
And so, my boy, Aurva cast the fire born of his anger into the sea. And in the sea it consumes the waters.
58. Having become the great horse-head[8] known to all knowers of the Vedas, it vomits forth that fire and drinks up the waters in the ocean.
59. Therefore, Parāśara, great among the wise, since you know the highest law (*dharma*), you should not destroy the worlds either.

[8] See Wendy D. O'Flaherty, "The Submarine Mare in the Mythology of Śiva," *JRAS* no. 1 (1971), 9–27.

RĀMA (=R)
(*Mbh* III.115–17)

1. Yudhiṣṭhira said:
   You are an attendant of the mighty Rāma Jāmadagnya. You were a witness to all the deeds of his early career.
2. Tell me how, and for what reason, Rāma defeated all the kṣatriyas in battle.
3. Akṛtavraṇa said:
   There was a great and mighty king in Kanyakubja called Gādhi who went to dwell in the forest.
4. While he was dwelling in the forest, a daughter like a celestial nymph (*apsaras*) was born to him, and Ṛcīka, the Bhārgava, asked for her hand.
5. Then the king said to that brahman, whose vows were fulfilled, "There is a certain custom in our family that was established by our ancestors.
6. Know, great brahman, that the bride price is one thousand swift white horses, whose ears are black on one side.[1]

[1] *ekataḥśyāmakarṇa*: Nīl. explains the bahuvrīhi as follows: *bahiḥ śyāmāḥ antarā raktāḥ karṇā yeṣāṃ te* . . . That is to say, the outside of the ears is black while the inside is red. This term, which occurs in another variant (*Mbh* XIII.4.14) might also mean "with one black ear."

7. But Bhārgava, you are not one to be addressed with the word, 'Give.' This daughter of mine is [in any case] to be given to a great personage such as you."
8. Ṛcīka said:
"I will give you a thousand swift horses whose ears are black on one side. Let your daughter become my wife."
9. Having agreed, O king, he said to Varuṇa, "Give me, for a bride price, one thousand swift white horses, whose ears are black on one side."
10. Then Varuṇa gave him the thousand horses, and the place from which the horses came was called Aśvatīrtha, "horse shrine."
11. And so at Kanyakubja on the Ganges, Gādhi, having received the thousand horses and having seen the gods who made up the groom's party,[2] gave him his daughter.
12. The great brahman Ṛcīka, having obtained his wife in accordance with dharma, sported with her according to his wish and pleasure.
13. When, O king, the marriage had been performed, the greatest of the Bhṛgus [Bhṛgu himself] came, wishing to see him and his wife. Having seen his son he was greatly pleased.
14. Then the couple did homage to the seated guru, who was revered by the hosts of the gods, prostrated themselves, and remained in an attitude of respect.
15. Pleased, the lord Bhṛgu said to his daughter-in-law,

[2] Nīl. glosses *janyāḥ* as *varapakṣīyāḥ*, "belonging to the groom's party." This is yet another example of the special intimacy between the gods and the Bhārgavas. See also v. 25, where the gods are said to be in Jamadagni's power.

"Choose a boon, lovely one. I shall give you what you desire."

16. She propitiated the guru for the sake of a son, and he was gracious to her and to her mother.[3]
17. Bhṛgu said:
"In order to conceive sons, you and your mother, having bathed, should embrace different trees; she the aśvattha, you the udumbara."[4]
18. But in the embracing, O king, they made a switch. Bhṛgu, returning after some time, was aware of the exchange.
19. Then the glorious Bhṛgu said to Satyavatī, his daughter-in-law, "Your son will be a brahman whose conduct will be that of a kṣatriya.
20. The mighty son of your mother will be a kṣatriya who

[3] In all four *Mbh* versions of the birth of Rāma and Viśvāmitra, Satyavatī's mother tampers with the boon. Only one of these versions, however, the Anuś, attempts to fully explain her motives. There, in a realistic and amusing passage (*Mbh* XIII.4.30–33), the mother, having solicited a boon for herself from her son-in-law, reflects that he would most likely have granted the best son to his own wife. By means of an emotional appeal, she selfishly prevails upon her devoted daughter to switch boons. The Śānti version is ambiguous in this respect, stating that the mother gave her own specially sanctified food to Satyavatī but that she appropriated the latter's "unknowingly" (*Mbh* XII.49.15). Later in the passage Ṛcīka tells Satyavatī that she has been "cheated" by her mother (XII.49.18). A brief reference later in the Anuś states simply that "two women" are the cause of the crossed characteristics of the two heroes (*Mbh* XII.56.13, = CK 35). Our version makes no effort to explain. The real reason for the introduction of the mother and the switch motif is, or course, the desire to trace to a single cause the two most important examples of social aberrance in the traditional literature.

[4] After this verse the Citr. ed. (III.115.36) inserts the additional condition of a switch of two specially prepared *carus*, or special portions of porridge. The motif of the carus is used instead of the tree motif in the Śānti version (*Mbh* XII.49.8 ff.). In the Anuś version (*Mbh* XIII.4.17–18), both motifs appear.

will behave like a brahman, a great hero who will follow the path of the holy men."

21. [Satyavatī said:] "No, do not let my son be like that! If you please, let it be my grandson." "Let it be so" [said Bhṛgu]. Thus, O Pāṇḍava, she was comforted.
22. In the course of time, she gave birth to a son, Jamadagni, a scion of the Bhārgavas, full of power and brilliance.
23. Increasing in knowledge of the Vedas, this powerful man surpassed many ṛṣis.
24. The entire *dhanurveda* [science of arms], along with the four types of missiles, revealed itself to him, who was as brilliant as the sun.

(116.1–29) Akṛtavraṇa said:

25. The great ascetic Jamadagni, given over to the study of the Vedas, performed austerities and brought the gods under his control.
26. O king, he approached the king Prasenajit and asked him for Reṇukā. The king gave her to him.
27. Now the scion of the Bhārgavas, having taken Reṇukā as his wife, performed penances with the agreeable girl in his hermitage.
28. Four sons were born to her, with Rāma making a fifth. Rāma, although the last born (*jaghanyaja*), was not the least of them (*ajaghanya*).
29. Once, when all the sons had gone to gather fruits, the pious Reṇukā went to bathe.
30. But as she was returning, she happened to see Citraratha, the king of Mārtikāvataka.
31. Seeing him, richly endowed and lotus-garlanded, sporting with his wife in the water, Reṇukā desired him.

32. Having lost her senses because of that infidelity, she was soaked in the water:[5] and when she returned in terror to the hermitage, her husband understood.
33. Seeing her fallen from virtue, bereft of her spiritual power and her beauty,[6] the mighty sage condemned her with the word "Shame."
34. Then came Rumaṇvat, the eldest son of Jamadagni, followed by Suṣeṇa, Vasu, and Viśvāvasu.
35. The lord then asked them all, in turn, to kill their mother. Stunned and confused, they said nothing.
36. Then in his anger he cursed them and, cursed, they lost their wits. Like beasts or birds, they immediately became like those bereft of reason.
37. Then Rāma, slayer of heroes, returned to the hermitage. Furious, the great sage addressed him:
38. "Slay this sinful mother, son. Have no fear." Then taking his axe, Rāma cut off his mother's head.
39. O king, the great Jamadagni's anger vanished all at once. He was pleased, and said this:
40. "Son, you have done this difficult task in accordance

[5] The intent of the phrase *klinnāmbhasi* is not clear. In what sense is Reṇukā soaked in water? Is the idea that, having "lost her senses" (become *vicetanā*) she falls in the water? Perhaps, but as she was bathing anyway she would already have been wet. Some later purāṇic versions have an elaborate story, perhaps based on this phrase, according to which Reṇukā, through her chastity, fidelity, and austerity, had achieved the power either to bathe without getting wet or to roll water back to the ashram in a ball. She loses this power and so Jamadagni comes to know of her erotic fantasy. This story seems clearly derivative and moreover would be a slight on the sage's powers of omniscience. Nīl. gives a purely erotic interpretation, citing the following curious verse: *sundaraṃ puruṣaṃ dṛṣtvā bhrātaram pitaraṃ sutam/yonir dravati nārīṇāṃ satyaṃ satyaṃ janārdana//*"When she sees a handsome man, whether it be her brother, father, or even a son, a woman's cunt grows wet. This is the truth, the truth, Janārdana."

[6] *brāhmyā lakṣmyā vivarjitām*: Brāhmī is the energy she had acquired as a brahman's wife through her chastity. Lakṣmī may be taken as her beauty and splendor as a princess.

with my words. Choose boons, O knower of dharma, as many as your heart desires."

41. He chose the restoration of his mother and her forgetfulness of her murder; his absolution from the sin[7] and the restoration of his brothers to their natural state.

42. He chose long life, and to be unrivaled in battle. The great ascetic Jamadagni granted all these boons.

43. Now, lord, once, when all [Jamadagni's] sons had gone out, the hero Kārtavīrya, the lord of Anūpa, came by. The ṛṣi's wife honored him when he had reached the hermitage.

44–45. But he was infatuated with his martial pride, and took no notice of the respect done him. Behaving violently, he abducted, by force, the calf of the cow whose milk was used for the oblations, and who was wailing. He broke down the great trees.

46. Rāma's father told him when he returned, and seeing the weeping cow, Rāma was seized by wrath.

47. Given over to fury, that Bhārgava, the destroyer of his foes, pursued Kārtavīrya and overcame him in battle.

48. Taking his shining bow, lord, he severed [Kārtavīrya's] thousand arms, which were like iron bars, with sharp crescent-arrows.

49. Then Arjuna's kinsmen were enraged with Rāma, and they ran to Jamadagni, who was alone in his hermitage.

50. They slew the great sage, who made no resistance, merely crying "Rāma" repeatedly like one who has no protector.

[7] The sin is, of course, *strīvadha*, woman-slaying.

51. Then, O Yudhiṣṭhira, the warlike sons of Kārtavīrya, having slain Jamadagni with arrows, went off as they had come.
52. When they had gone, and when Jamadagni was dead, the scion of the Bhṛgu race returned to the hermitage with sacrificial fuel in his hand.
53. Seeing his father, who did not deserve such a state,[8] fallen into the grip of death, the hero was stricken with grief, and he lamented.

(117.1–15) Rāma said:

54. "It is my fault, father, that you were slain with arrows like a deer in the wood by these lowly fools, the kinsmen of Kārtavīrya.
55. Father, how is such a death fitting for a knower of dharma, a follower of the path of truth who never harmed any creature.
56. What a foul deed they have done to have slain you with hundreds of sharp arrows, an old man immersed in austerities, offering no resistance.
57. What will these shameless fellows tell their friends and ministers after killing a single, unresisting sage?"

Akṛtavraṇa said:

58. Lamenting thus at length, mournfully, O king, the great ascetic performed all the funeral rites for his father.
59. Rāma, the conqueror of his enemies' strongholds, cremated his father and then vowed the slaughter of all the kṣatriyas, O Bhārata.

[8] *anarhantam*: Nīl., unlike Rāma, has not forgotten the murder of Reṇukā. Regarding this verse he notes: "The gist of it is that because of the crime of killing his wife, he suffered such, i.e., a violent death himself." Notice also that in v. 55 Rāma refers to Jamadagni as one who had never harmed anyone.

60. Enraged, the valorous and exceedingly mighty hero took his weapon and single-handedly like death incarnate killed the sons of Kārtavīrya.
61. Rāma, the best of warriors, slaughtered all their followers too, O best of kṣatriyas.
62. Twenty-one times, lord, he cleared the earth of kṣatriyas and in the Samantapañcaka region he made five lakes of blood.
63. In them, the upholder of the Bhṛgu race made libations to his deceased ancestors. Then Rāma had a vision of Ṛcīka himself who stopped him.[9]
64. Then by means of a great sacrifice, the glorious son of Jamadagni satisfied the lord of the gods and presented the earth to the sacrificial priests.
65. And he made a golden altar ten fathoms[10] wide and nine high and gave it to the great Kaśyapa.
66. With Kasyapa's consent the brahmans divided it in pieces (*khaṇḍaśas*), for which reason, O king, they are called *khāṇḍavāyanas*.
67. Having presented the earth to the great Kaśyapa, that man of great valor dwells on this lordly Mahendra peak.
68. Thus did the hostility arise between him and the kṣatriyas of this world, and thus was the earth conquered by the glorious Rāma.

[9] Ṛcīka stops Rāma from further killing. This is a closely parallel motif to the Bhārgava pitṛs' intervention in the Aurva episode. The appearance of a single, named, ancestor here is in keeping with the contrast between the episodes; the Aurva story deals with groups (Bhṛgus, kṣatriyas, pitṛs), while the Rāma story deals with individuals (Jamadagni, Kārtavīrya, Ṛcīka, etc.).

[10] The unit of measurement here is the *vyāma*, measured between the fingertips of a man with arms extended to either side.

ŚUKRA AND KACA (=ŚK) (*Mbh* I.71.1–58)

Janamejaya said:

1. How did our ancestor, Yayāti, tenth in line of descent from Prajāpati, obtain Śukra's daughter, who was extremely hard to gain?
2. I want to hear that in great detail, O great sage. Recount to me the scions of the race of Puru in order, individually.

Vaiśampāyana said:

3. Yayāti was a royal sage (*rājarṣi*) equal in glory to the king of the gods. Śukra and Vṛṣaparvan chose[1] him in accordance with ancient custom.
4. That I will relate to you, since you ask, Janamejaya, that union of Devayānī and Yayāti, a descendant of Nahuṣa.
5. Mutual rivalry arose between the gods and the asuras

[1] *vavrāte*: Nīl. supplies *jāmātṛtveneti śeṣaḥ*; i.e., they chose him as their son-in-law. The reference is to the marriage, later on in the story, of Yayāti to Devayānī and Śarmiṣṭhā—daughters, respectively, of Śukra and Vṛṣaparvan.

over the lordship of the three worlds with their contents, both moving and fixed.

6. Then the gods, desirous of victory, chose the sage (*muni*) Āṅgirasa [Bṛhaspati] as their chaplain (*purohita*) for the purpose of sacrificing; the others chose Uśanas [Kāvya, Śukra]. The two brahmans were continually engaged in fierce rivalry.
7. Having recourse to the power of a spell (*vidyā*) Kāvya brought back to life whichever demons (*dānavas*) the gods slew in battle. Rising up again, they gave battle to the gods.
8. But the wise Bṛhaspati did not revive the gods whom the asuras slew in the front line of battle,
9. For he did not know the revivifying spell that the mighty Kāvya knew; and so the gods became extremely dejected.
10. Then the gods, trembling in fear of Uśanas Kāvya, approached Kaca, the eldest son of Bṛhaspati, and said:
11. "Favor us, the sharers;[2] render us great assistance. Obtain that spell which resides in the glorious brahman Śukra, and you shall immediately become our partner (*bhāgabhāk*).

[2] *bhajamānān bhajasvāsmān*: The gods refer, suggestively, to themselves as sharers of the sacrifice. The play on the root √*bhaj* is complicated by the numerous meanings the root can have. Thus, for example, the phrase could be translated as "favor us who honor [you], serve [you]," etc. However, in this context, it would appear that the gods are seeking to enlist Kaca's help by offering him a share *bhāga*, √*bhaj*) in the sacrifice. This type of offer is common in the Brāhmaṇa literature where it recurs in the same context. This interpretation is reinforced by the promise made in v. 11 to make Kaca a *bhāgabhāk*, "a sharer of a share" or partner.

12. You can find this brahman in the vicinity of Vṛṣaparvan. There he protects[3] the demons and not the gods.
13. As a young man, you will be able to win over this seer and also Devayānī, the great man's beloved daughter.
14. You alone can please them. And when Devayānī has been pleased by your virtue, courtesy, sweetness, good conduct, and restraint, you will surely get the spell."
15. Then, Kaca, the son of Bṛhaspati, agreed; and he went off, honored by the gods, to Vṛṣaparvan's place.
16. Kaca went swiftly, O king, as he was sent by the gods. He saw Śukra in the city of the asura king and said these words:
17. "I am Kaca, grandson of the ṛṣi Āṅgirasa and son of Bṛhaspati himself. Accept me as your pupil.
18. Accept me. With you as my guru I will adopt the student's life (*brahmacarya*) for a thousand years."

Śukra said:

19. "You are indeed welcome Kaca. I accept your proposal. I shall honor you, who are worthy of

[3] *rakṣate dānavāṃṣ tatra na sa rakṣaty adānavān/* This is a rather perplexing locution. In the first place, one wonders why √*rakṣ*, normally conjugated in parasmaipada, first appears in the ātmanepada, and then why the usage is not consistent in the half-verse. Nīl.'s explanation is as follows: *rakṣata/karmavyatihāre tañ/śukraṃ hi dānavā rakṣanti ayam asmatto mā gād iti/śukras tu tān rakṣaty eva/adānavān devān/mṛtasaṃjīvinyā na rakṣati//* A rough translation would be: "The middle ending is used in the case of mutual action. The dānavas guard Śukra, [saying,] 'Let him not go away from us!' Śukra, however, protects them as well. He does not protect the non-dānavas, i.e., the gods, by means of the mṛtasaṃjīvinī[vidyā]." *Dānava* and *daitya* are synonymous with *asura*, demon.

honor, that Bṛhaspati may be honored."

Vaiśampāyana said:

20. Kaca agreed and undertook that vow taught him by Uśanas son of Kavi, Śukra himself.
21. He accepted the period of the vow as previously mentioned and pleased his teacher and Devayānī, O Bhārata.
22. At the beginning, the young man, in the prime of youth, won over Devayānī, singing, dancing, playing instruments, always delighting her.
23. He charmed the youthful Devayānī with flowers, fruits, and various favors.
24. The wanton girl (*lalanā*)[4] Devayānī, being sung to, in turn secretly served that brahman while he kept his vows and restrictions.
25. So five hundred years passed[5] while Kaca was engaged in his vow. Then the dānavas, recognizing Kaca,
26. and seeing him tending cows alone in a deserted forest, slew him in anger because of their hatred for Bṛhaspati and in order to preserve the spell. When they had killed him they cut him to pieces and fed him to the jackals.
27. Then the cows returned to their stalls without their

[4] *lalanā*: She does not, however, compromise Kaca's chastity; see v. 38.

[5] *atīyuḥ*: Nīl. takes *dānavāḥ* and not *varṣaśatāni* as the subject. He thus takes it in the sense of "transgress": *brāhmaṇasyāvadhyatvam atikrāntavanta ity arthaḥ*/That is to say, they (the dānavas) violated the prohibition on the killing of brahmans. This interpretation is ingenious but unconvincing. Note that in the text the issue of brahmahatyā is not raised in connection with the demons' murder of Kaca, but with regard to Śukra's ingestion of him (see v. 39).

herdsman. Devayānī saw the cows returning from the forest without Kaca and after a time she said,

28. "You have not offered the evening oblation to the fire (*agnihotra*) and the sun has set, lord. The cows have come back without a herdsman, and, father, Kaca is nowhere to be seen.
29. Surely Kaca has died or been murdered, father. Truly I tell you I cannot live without him."
Śukra said:
30. I will revive the dead boy with the words "Come here!"
Vaiśaṃpāyana said:
31. Then using the saṃjīvanī spell, he called Kaca.[6] Summoned then by the spell, Kaca appeared unharmed. When questioned by the brahman's daughter, he replied, "I was killed."
32. The brahman [Kaca] happened to go once more to the forest at Devayānī's request to gather flowers. The dānavas saw him.
33. The demons killed him a second time. They burnt and ground him to a powder and gave him to that brahman [Śukra] in his wine.
34. Once more, Devayānī spoke to her father: "Father, Kaca went out to gather flowers and now he is nowhere to be seen."
35. Śukra said:
"Daughter, Bṛhaspati's son has gone by the path of

[6] The Citr. ed. and several MSS insert the following line after 31a–b: *bhittvā bhittvā śarīrāṇi vṛkāṇāṃ sa vinirgataḥ* [v. l. *viniṣpatat*]: "Splitting open the bodies of the wolves, he came out." This interpolation presages Kaca's emergence from the belly of his guru.

the dead. Even though he was revived by the spell, he has been killed again. What am I to do?

36. Do not grieve so, Devayānī, do not cry. One like you should not grieve for a mortal.[7] All the gods and the whole world bow before this change [death] when it comes."

37. "How should I not grieve and weep for him whose grandfather was the venerable Āṅgiras and whose father is the ascetic Bṛhaspati, the son and grandson of ṛṣis.

38. He was chaste and ascetic, always upright and deft in his actions. I will not eat. I will follow Kaca's path, for the handsome Kaca was dear to me, father."

39. Śukra said:
"Doubtless these asuras, who slay my innocent student, hate me. These savages want to make me as a non-brahman. For they have already accomplished it. Would not this be the consequence of this sin? For who, including Indra, would not be consumed by brahman-slaying?"

40. Vaiśaṃpāyana said:
Pressed by Devayānī, Kāvya the great sage quickly summoned Kaca the son of Bṛhaspati once more.

41. Summoned with that spell but fearful of his guru, he

[7] This passage is curious in the light of the close association of the Āṅgirasas and the Bhārgavas (see chapter 4). Śukra is evidently implying that his own daughter is somehow of higher status than Bṛhaspati's son; perhaps even that the former is immortal and the latter mortal. The situation and especially the dialogue between Kaca and Devayānī in adhyāya 72 is reminiscent in several ways of the famous Yama-Yamī sūkta of *RV* X.10. It is possible that the same motif underlies both passages. See Goldman, "Mortal Man and Immortal Woman."

spoke haltingly in [Kāvya's] belly. Śukra said to him, "Having come by what path do you stand in my belly? Speak, brahman."

42. Kaca said:

"Through your grace, my memory has not deserted me; I remember everything just as it occurred. Nor would there be thus any diminution of my spiritual power. Therefore I endure this dreadful suffering.

43. The asuras killed me, burned me, ground me up, and put me in your wine, O Kāvya. How, in your presence, could the magic power of the asuras surpass that of the brahmans?"

Śukra said:

44. "What now can I do to please you, daughter? Kaca may live only through my death. Not otherwise than by the splitting open of my belly may Kaca, issuing forth from me, be seen, Devayānī."

Devayānī said:

45. "Two sorrows, like fires, consume me: the destruction of Kaca and your death. In the destruction of Kaca there is no happiness. If you are killed, I cannot live."

Śukra said:

46. "You have been completely sucessful, O son of Bṛhaspati, since Devayānī is devoted to you, who are devoted [to her?]. Take this life-giving spell, if you are not Indra in Kaca's form.[8]

[8] *indraḥ kacarupī*: The reference is to the well-known prediliction of the king of the gods for assuming various shapes to accomplish his ends. See note to C 64. Nīl. explains: "The intention is, 'If you are Indra, then I will cause you to grow old inside my belly." (Comm. to Citr. ed. I.76.) This is yet another allusion to the superiority of the Bhṛgus to the gods.

47. No one but a brahman[9] could issue forth again alive from my belly. Therefore take the spell.
48. Coming forth from this body, my boy, become a cherished son, and cherish me. Observe the righteous mode of conduct, since, as a wise man, you have obtained the spell from your teacher."

Vaiśampāyana said:

49. Taking the spell from his guru, the handsome Kaca split open [Śukra's] belly and came out on the brahman's right side, like the moon at the end of the bright half of the month.
50. Seeing that storehouse of the Vedas fallen, Kaca, having obtained the spell that he had won, made reverent salutation and raised up the dead man. Then Kaca spoke thus to his guru:
51. "Those who do not revere a venerable guru, a teacher of the highest truth and a treasure-house of the fourfold treasure,[10] go to evil worlds, devoid of glory."[11]

Vaiśaṃpāyana said:

52. Given over to illusion from the drinking of the wine,

[9] *brāhmaṇaṃ varjayitvā*: Nīl. in his commentary on this verse raises once more the issue of brahmahatyā. He says, *neti/tvaṃ tu brāhmaṇatvād avadhyo mamety arthaḥ/* The verse beginning *na* etc. means, "Because you are a brahman, I cannot kill you." (Comm. to Citr. ed. 1.76.59.)

[10] The fourfold treasure, according to Nīl. (who, incidentally, accepts a variant reading, *labdhavidyāḥ*, for *caturanvayānām*) are four actions associated with teaching.

[11] This marks the end of Śukra's role as the wielder of the saṃjīvanī vidyā in the Yayāti episode. He continues, of course, to play a critical role in the remainder of the lengthy saga, but in ways that are not relevant to this study. I might, however, note one point of interest. In adhyāya 72, Kaca rejects Devayānī's plea that he marry her on the grounds that, since he has been "born" from Śukra, they are, in a sense, brother and sister. As a result she curses him so that the spell

and to a terrible clouding of his wits, deluded by the wine, [Śukra] drank his beloved Kaca even though he perceived him.

53. The mighty Uśanas, afflicted with grief and desirous of doing that which would be beneficial to brahmans, himself uttered these words, as he was fearful of the drinking of wine:
54. "From this day forward, whatever foolish brahman shall, in his delusion, drink wine, shall be condemned in this world and the next as one devoid of righteousness (*dharma*) and as a slayer of brahmans.
55. I have established this prohibition as a limit to the righteous behavior (*dharma*) of brahmans in all the worlds. Let it be heard by all men, gods, and good brahmans attentive to their gurus."
56. When he had spoken thus, that great and limitless storehouse of the treasures of austerity summoned the dānavas whose minds had been confused by fate and said:
57. "You are fools, I tell you, dānavas. Kaca has been successful and will dwell with me. Having obtained the great saṃjīvanī spell, and having become a brahman, he is now Brahman's equal in power."
58. After dwelling with his guru for a thousand years, Kaca took leave of his master, and wished to go to the abode of the gods.

---

shall never work for him. The point is that even though Kaca's plan has succeeded, there is no real use of the vidyā by anyone save the Bhṛgu sage. Later on, Śukra is closely involved with the motif of the restoration of youth, which forms the nexus of the Yayāti story (*Mbh* I.78.30 to I.79.30).

ŚUKRA AND THE ASURAS (=ŚA) (*MatsyaP* 47)[1]

(47.61–126) 1. When, in the course of time, the three worlds were taken[2] from Prahlāda and were ruled in turn by Indra, Śukra[3] deserted the asuras and went over to the gods.

[1] In this, the one major episode on which I have relied heavily that does not appear in the *Mbh*, I encountered numerous problems not encountered in the other passages because of the lack of a critical edition. In difficult cases, I have compared the variant readings offered by the editors of the ASS texts of both the *MatsyaP* and the closely parallel version that appears at *PadmaP* V.13.202 ff. Where I have ventured to suggest the adoption of a given variant or emendation, I have done so chiefly with regard to what appears to me to make for better Sanskrit, better sense, or both. Such suggestions are not, obviously, to be taken as having any text-critical basis. A more scientific analysis awaits the publication of a critical edition of the *MatsyaP*, an edition that has been undertaken by Professor Raghavan.

The *PadmaP* is of later composition than the *MatsyaP*; so when it offers preferable readings, these may as well be emendations as evidence of a better MSS tradition.

[2] *hate*: The *PadmaP* reading *hṛte*, found also in the ASS ed.'s MS "ga," makes better sense.

[3] *śukraḥ*: The ASS MSS "ga" and "ca" share with the *PadmaP* the variant *yajñaḥ* ("sacrifice").

2. The sons of Diti [the asuras] summoned Kāvya, who had gone over to the gods, at the sacrifice.[4] "Have you returned to the sacrifice, abandoning our kingdom before our very eyes?
3. We cannot remain here. We shall enter the underworld (Rasātala) at once!" Addressed in this fashion, he replied to the discouraged daityas, soothing them with his words:
4. "Do not be afraid. I will support you, asuras, with my own power. Mantras, herbs, essences, and vast wealth,
5. all this is mine. Only a fraction belongs to these gods. I will give you all this, which I have kept for your sake."
6. The gods, seeing [the asuras] favored by the wise Kāvya, consulted together in their desire to get the better of them:
7. "This Kāvya means to take all this from us by force. Very well then; let's go quickly before he instructs them.[5]
8. We'll massacre them and send the survivors to Hell!" Then the raging gods attacked the dānavas.
9. As they [the asuras] were being slaughtered, they ran straight to Kāvya. Kāvya saw them quickly put to flight by the gods.
10. Even though they were taunted by the asuras, the gods withdrew in the face of Kāvya's protection.[6]

[4] *yajñe devān*: *PadmaP* 204 tries to clarify: *hṛtaṃ maghavatā rājyaṃ tyaktvā yajñaḥ surān gataḥ*/"Maghavan [Indra] has taken [our] kingdoms. The sacrifice, having left us, has gone over to the gods."

[5] *vyavartayati*: *PadmaP* 209 has *cyāvayeta vai*, "he will cause [us] to fall."

[6] *rakṣāṃ kāvyena*: *PadmaP* 211's *rakṣakāryena saṃhṛtya devebhyas tān surārditān* ("Holding them, who were harried by the gods, back from the gods out of his duty to protect them") seems somewhat more lucid.

Seeing Kāvya standing there, they left the asuras alone without the least hesitation.

11. Then, after deep reflection, the brahman Kāvya, recalling the events of the past, addressed the demons with beneficial words of advice:
12. "With three paces the Dwarf took all the three worlds from you. Bali was bound, while Jambha and Virocana were slain.
13. The great asuras were slaughtered by the gods in twelve battles. By one means or another the best of you have been killed off.
14. Only a few of you remain. In my opinion there should be no fighting. I advise stratagem. Hold on until the situation has changed.
15. I shall go to Mahādeva in order to obtain mantras conducive to victory. When I have obtained these favorable spells from Mahādeva, we shall again do battle[7] with the gods and you will win."
16. Then the asuras, having discussed the matter, said to the gods, "We have all laid down our arms.[8] We have neither armor nor chariots.
17. Clothed in garments of bark, we shall perform penances in the forest." Hearing this speech of Prahlāda, the gods took it for the truth.
18. Since the daityas had laid down their arms, the gods, free from anxiety, went home delighted.

[7] *yudhyāmahe*: *PadmaP* 217's *saṃyotsyadhve* is an attempt to keep parallelism between the two verbs by keeping them both in the second person plural. The *MatsyaP* reading, as I have noted above, lends, intentionally or otherwise, a greater aura of altruism to the character of Kāvya insofar as he offers (via use of the first person plural) to help in the fight but appears to decline a share in the spoils (second person, *prāpsyatha*).

[8] *nyastaśastrā vayam*. Note the facile hypocrisy of the demons and the startling gullibility of the gods.

19. Soon after, Kāvya told the asuras, "Wait a while, engaged in penances. Do not worry. Time will effect our purpose.
20. Wait for me, dānavas, in my father's hermitage." Having thus instructed the asuras, Kāvya approached Mahādeva.
Śukra said:
21. "O god, I desire such mantras as Bṛhaspati does not possess, mantras for the conquest of the gods and the triumph of the asuras."
22. Addressed in this way, the god replied, "Perform an act of penance, Bhārgava. If you will inhale dense smoke with your head downward for a full one thousand years, you shall have the mantras."
23. "So be it." Assenting thus, Śukra, scion of the Bhṛgu race, touched the god's feet and said, "I will undertake this vow as you have instructed me this day, Lord."
24. Then the god produced a very smoky fire in a pit. Śukra approached it and dwelt there as a brahmacārin for the sake of the mantras and the welfare of the asuras.
25. The gods became aware of the fact that the asuras had abandoned their kingdom merely as a stratagem. So they armed and armored themselves and, placing Bṛhaspati at their head, rushed furiously upon the demons in their moment of weakness.
26. When the asuras saw that the gods had once more taken up arms, they leaped up in terror and spoke to them:
27. "Since we are weaponless and our preceptor is engaged in austerities, you gentlemen promised us security. Now you come intending to kill us!

28. We have abandoned our weapons, O gods, and live here without our teacher. We undertake no actions and have no possessions but our garments of bark and antelope skin.
29. By no means can we defeat the gods in battle. Without a fight, then, let us go and take refuge with Kāvya's mother.
30. Let us avert this danger until our guru returns. When Śukra comes back we will arm and fight."
31. Discussing the matter among themselves, the terrified asuras approached Kāvya's mother for protection. She banished their fear:
32. "Fear not! Fear not! Abandon fear, O dānavas. You should have no fear while in my presence."
33. Now when the gods saw that the asuras were being protected by her, they assaulted them violently, not pausing to consider their relative strength.
34. The lady, seeing the asuras assailed by the gods, was furious. She said, "I shall deprive the gods of their leader."
35. She assembled all the requisite things and cast a spell on Indra. This lady, a great ascetic and a powerful sorceress, immobilized him.
36. The gods,[9] when they saw Indra paralyzed and subjected to her will, were struck dumb and fled in terror.
37. When the hosts of the gods had fled, Viṣṇu said to Indra, "Enter into me, Indra. I will carry you."
38–39. When he had been addressed in this manner, Indra entered Viṣṇu. The lady was infuriated at seeing him

[9] I have adopted *PadmaP* 240's *devāś ca* in place of the obviously erroneous *devāṃś ca*.

protected by Viṣṇu. She said, "I will burn you up, and Viṣṇu with you, O Maghavan, right in front of all these beings.[10] You shall behold the power of my austerities!"

40. She[11] overpowered both gods, Indra and Viṣṇu. Viṣṇu asked Indra, "How shall we free ourselves?"

41. Indra said, "Kill her before she burns us up, Lord. I am even worse off than you. Kill her quickly!"

42. Now, in considering her, Viṣṇu resorted to the sin of slaying a woman. Then he called to mind his discus to save him.

43. Viṣṇu was frightened and recognizing her hostile intentions, he acted quickly. Enraged, he cut off her head with his weapon, through fear.

44. The lord Bhṛgu, when he saw this terrible act of killing a woman, was enraged. He cursed Viṣṇu for killing his wife.

45. "Since you, a knower of dharma, have slain a woman who is not to be slain, may you be born in this world seven times among men."

46. Therefore, because of that curse, he is born in the world again and again among men, when dharma is threatened, for the welfare of the world.

47–48. When he had cursed Viṣṇu, Bhṛgu took the head and body and joined them, saying: "Viṣṇu killed you, my

[10] *eṣām*: This, not the variant *eṣā* (*PadmaP* 243), is the correct reading. It construes with the genitive plurals in the second half of the verse to make up an example of *anādare ṣaṣṭhī*. In the whole passage dealing with the confrontation of Kāvya's mother and the gods, the *MatsyaP* readings of the printed text are generally superior to those in the *PadmaP* text.

[11] *tayā*: In fact they have not actually been overcome "by her" as yet. The *PadmaP* reading (v. 244) *bhayābhibhūtau*, "overcome with fear," may be more to the point.

lady; I restore you to life." Then he[12] joined her with her head once more and said, "Live!

49. If I know dharma fully, and if I have acted in accordance with it, if I am speaking the truth, may you come to life again by the power of that truth."
50. He then sprinkled her with cool water and said, "Live!" Even as he was speaking,[13] she came to life again.
51. When all the beings saw her risen as if from sleep, they cried "Excellent, excellent!" on all sides.
52. It was a great wonder to those divinities who observed it that the lady was thus restored by Bhṛgu.
53. When Indra saw Bhṛgu calmly restore his wife to life, he became sleepless and could find no respite from his fear of Kāvya. He spoke to Jayantī.
54. After some thought, the wise Indra addressed his daughter; "This Kāvya is carrying out a terrible vow for the good of our enemies. Daughter, this sage alarms me.
55. Go and win him over[14] by the attentive performance of such pleasant ministrations as will lessen his weariness.
56. Propitiate this brahman Kāvya so that he is pleased. Go! I give you to him. Make this effort for my sake."
57. Jayantī, when she was spoken to in this way, acceded to her father's wishes. She went to the place at which [Śukra] was engaged in severe austerities.

[12] *asau*: *PadmaP* 251's *pāṇau*, "in [his] hand" is more closely descriptive of the actual method whereby Bhṛgu restores his wife.

[13] *tasya*: *PadmaP*'s *tasmin* (v.254) is to be preferred, as it completes the *sati saptamī* construction, *abhivyāhṛte tasmin*.

[14] *saṃsādhayasva*: *PadmaP* 260 has *mohaya*, "infatuate."

58. She saw him being held upside down by a yakṣa,[15] inhaling the dense smoke produced in the fire pit.

59. When she saw him hanging there, emaciated but lustrous and calm from his meditation on the supreme being,[16] she did what her father had told her with respect to Kāvya.

60. The sweet-voiced girl praised him with fitting words and dwelt there for many years tending him with gentle massage of the limbs and other services such as are suitable to one engaged in a vow of austerity.

61. When the terrible thousand-year smoke penance was completed Bhava [Śiva] was pleased and offered Kāvya a boon.

62–66. Mahādeva said:

"No one excepting you alone has ever fulfilled this vow. Therefore, you alone will surpass the gods in austerity, intelligence, learning, power, and glory. You will obtain whatever you desire, O brahman, son of the Bhṛgu race. But recite this [mantra] to no one. By means of it become superior to all beings." Having given these boons to Kāvya, Śiva also conferred upon him lordship, wealth, and invulnerability.

67. Kāvya was greatly delighted to receive these boons. In his joy he uttered a heavenly hymn of praise to Maheśvara. And so, upside down as he was, he

[15] *yakṣas* are a class of demigods, sometimes monstrous, sometimes benevolent.

[16] *pātyamānam*: Perhaps *PadmaP* 264's *yatamānam*, "exerting himself," is preferable. *svarūpadhyānaśamyantam*: for the *PadmaP*, the question of meditation does not arise. It reads (v. 264c) *śatrūpadhānaṃ śrāmyantam*, which presents difficulties of its own. Dr. V. W. Paranjpe of Poona University suggests emending to *śatrūpaghāte* . . . , "exerting himself for the destruction of his enemies."

praised Śiva. [*I omit here 128–68, which constitute Kāvya's Śivastotra, and continue with the narrative from v. 169.*]

(47.169–235) 68. The Sūta [bard] said:

"Having thus praised[17] the lord Nīlalohita [Śiva], the lord of the gods, he prostrated himself, bowed low, folded his hands, and remained silent.

69. Bhava was greatly pleased and touched Kāvya's body with his hand. Then, granting Śukra as long a vision as he desired, he disappeared on the spot.

70. When the lord of the gods had vanished, Kāvya saw Jayantī, his attendant, standing beside him, and he said, "To whom do you belong, fair one? Who are you that you share my hardships? Why do you attend me assiduously as though engaged in a severe penance yourself?

71. I am pleased, lovely lady, to be served with such modesty, devotion, and affection.

72. What do you desire, fair one? What wish of your shall I fulfill? I will grant your desire this day, no matter how difficult it may be."

73. When he had spoken to her in this way, she replied, "You know by the power of your austerity. O brahman, you know exactly what I want."

74. Perceiving the situation with his divine insight, he said to her, "You wish, charming one, to live with me for ten years.[18]

[17] *evaṃ ābhāṣya*: *PadmaP* (v. 272) has the same reading despite the fact that it has no Śivastotra recited by Śukra. This is one of the points that suggest the primacy of the *MatsyaP* version.

[18] *daśa varṣāṇi*: *PadmaP* 278 reads *śata* ("a hundred"), although *daśa* appears there as a variant reading. Perhaps, after all, ten years is too reasonable a time span for a purāṇic narrative.

75. You wish, beautiful lady, to be joined to me and invisible to all creatures. Yes, you may choose this boon of me, sweet-voiced one.
76. So be it! Let us go,[19] to our house, O bewitching one." Then, having returned to his home, he took Jayantī's hand in marriage.
77. So the Bhārgava lived with her for ten years, concealed by his magic power and invisible to all beings.
78. Now the sons of Diti, knowing that Kāvya had accomplished his purpose and returned, were delighted. Wishing to see him, they went to his home.
79. But when they got there they didn't see their guru, who was concealed by the power of illusion. Finding no trace of him,[20] they returned as they had come.
80. Bṛhaspati knew that Kāvya, in accordance with his boon, was detained for ten years in order to satisfy Jayantī.[21]
81. Realizing the daityas' weakness and urged by Indra, he assumed Kāvya's form and summoned them.
82. Then, when he saw that they had come, he said, "Welcome, my patrons! I have come for your benefit.

[19] *gacchāmaḥ*: Under the circumstances the dual *gacchāvaḥ* (*PadmaP* 280) seems preferable. On the other hand Kāvya uses the plural *naḥ*, which in an "honorific" sense is possible. *PadmaP* has *me*.

[20] *lakṣaṇaṃ tasya tad buddhvā*: The meaning of this as it stands is not clear. Although I have taken it to mean that the asuras found no sign of their guru, it would seem to say the opposite. If this is the case, then perhaps the *PadmaP* variant offers an explanation. *PadmaP* 284 reads: *lakṣaṇaṃ tasya saṃbudhya nādyāgacchati no guruḥ*/"Recognizing some sign [that he had been there] they said, 'Our teacher has not come today.'" Evidently they think he is out for the day.

[21] See *PadmaP* 285. From this point the *PadmaP* and *MatsyaP* versions diverge increasingly.

83. I will teach you the magical spells that I have obtained." Overjoyed, they approached him for the sake of the spells.
84. At the end of the ten years, Devayānī was born to Kāvya. He then decided to go and see his patrons.
85. "O lovely wife, I am going to see my patrons."
86. Addressed thus, she replied, "Attend upon your devotees, O man of great vows. This is the duty of good men and I will not obstruct your duty (*dharma*)."
87. He went there and saw the asuras being deceived by the clever preceptor of the gods, who had taken his form. He spoke to them:
88. "Know that I am your Kāvya, who has gratified the Lord Śiva. Ach! Listen! You dānavas have been tricked."
89. Hearing him speak, they became confused. They were greatly astonished to see the two of them, one standing and one sitting.[22]
90. They were confused and could not understand at all. Then Kāvya spoke to the puzzled asuras.
91. "I am Kāvya, your preceptor. He is Aṅgiras, the preceptor of the gods. Follow me, daityas; abandon this Bṛhaspati."
92. When he had spoken to them in this way, the asuras regarded the two closely but were unable to discern any difference between them.

[22] *sthitāsīnau*: The *PadmaP* reading *āsīnaṃ bṛhaspatim* (v. 291) confirms the notion of the imposter seated in the attitude of an Indian teacher while the "real" Kāvya, having just come on the scene, is, naturally, standing. It is this distinction that leads the daityas to their fateful error. From v. 291 on, the *PadmaP* has a dialogue between Kāvya and Bṛhaspati that does not take place in the *MatsyaP*. Beyond this point there is no question of comparing readings as we have, in fact, two different texts.

93. Bṛhaspati, the great ascetic, calmly said, "I am Kāvya, your guru. He is Bṛhaspati in my form.

94–95. He is deluding you with my form, asuras." Hearing his words, they came together and said, "This lord has been instructing us for ten years. He is our guru. This brahman is trying to fool us."

96. Then the dānavas, deceived by long practice, believed [Bṛhaspati], and they prostrated themselves, doing him homage.

97. The demons, their eyes red with anger, said, "He is our guru and benefactor. You are not our guru. Go away!

98. Whether Bhārgava or Āṅgiras, this venerable one is our guru. We are under his tutelage. Well then, go away at once!"

99. Speaking thus, the asuras had recourse to Bṛhaspati and took no heed of the beneficial speech of Kāvya.

100. Bhārgava was furious at their arrogance. "Since you dānavas do not follow me, even though I have explained the matter to you,

101. you shall lose you wits and be defeated." Cursing them in this way, Kāvya departed as he had come.

102. Bṛhaspati, seeing the asuras cursed by Kāvya, was delighted at having accomplished his purpose and resumed his own form.

103. Having accomplished his purpose, and knowing that the asuras would be destroyed, he disappeared. When he had vanished, the asuras were dismayed.

104. "Alas," they said to one another, "we have been deceived. While we were facing this Āṅgirasa, he struck us from behind!"

105. Deceived on their own grounds by that imposture and the power of magic, the despondent dānavas, led by Prahlāda, ran quickly to follow Kāvya.

106–7. They overtook Kāvya and stood before him with lowered faces. Kāvya, seeing his patrons come again, said, "You rejected me even though I explained the matter to you. Because of this disrespect, you will be defeated."

108. Prahlāda then spoke to Śukra in a voice choked with tears: "Do not leave us, O Bhārgava.

109. O son of Bhṛgu, accept us as your disciples, your devotees, and your followers. We were deceived by the teacher of the gods while you were away. You must see, by that vision you have gained through penance, that we are devoted to you.

110. Son of Bhṛgu, if you show us no favor, if you despise us, we shall enter Rasātala this very day."

111. Kāvya recognized the true state of affairs and, moved by pity and compassion, restrained his anger and was appeased. He told them, "Do not fear. Do not go to Rasātala.

112. That which is inevitable would have come to pass, even had I been aware of it. Destiny is immutable and it is impossible to act in opposition to it.

113. You shall now regain the wits that you have lost. Only after having defeated the gods once more will you go to Pātāla.[23]

114. Brahman said that in the course of time, by his grace, you shall enjoy prosperous rule of the universe.

[23] Pātāla is an underworld decidedly more pleasant than the others such as Rasātala.

115. After ten full cosmic cycles (*yugas*), you will conquer the gods and rule. After that period of time Brahman has promised you sovereignty.
116. Lordship shall be returned to you in the age (*manvantara*) presided over by Manu Sāvarṇi. Your grandson, Bali, shall be lord of the worlds.
117. Viṣṇu himself promised this to your grandson. Such were his words when the worlds were taken away.
118. Since he was pleased with you, and appreciates your good conduct, Svayambhū [Brahman] has promised you all this.
119. The Lord told me that Bali will rule over the gods. Therefore, he [Bali] awaits the proper time, invisible to all creatures.
120. Svayambhū gave you this boon out of affection. Therefore, you and the asuras should patiently await your turn.
121. I was not able to tell you this before as I was forbidden by Brahman, knower of the future.
122. These two pupils of mine, the equals of Bṛhaspati, will support you in your conflict with the gods."
123. Addressed in this manner by the tireless Kāvya, Prahlāda and the asuras went away happy.
124. Having now heard of the inevitable future events discussed by Śukra, the asuras, in expectation of the promised victory, took up their armor and weapons and challenged the gods.
125. When the gods saw the asuras drawn up for battle, they equipped themselves fully and engaged them.
126. The battle between the gods and demons lasted a hundred years and the asuras were victorious. Then the gods conferred among themselves.

127. "If we invite those two [pupils of Kāvya] to the sacrifice, we shall defeat the asuras." So the gods summoned Śaṇḍa and Marka.

128. They called them to the sacrifice and said, "Brahmans, abandon the asuras. When we have defeated the demons together we will become your devotees."

129. When the gods had concluded this agreement with Śaṇḍa and Marka, they were victorious and the asuras were defeated.

130. The asuras, deserted by Śaṇḍa and Marka, were powerless. Thus were the daityas undone by the curse of Kāvya.

131. Deprived of a protector and overcome by Kāvya's curse, the asuras were driven off by the gods and entered Rasātala.

132–33. That is how the dānavas were rendered powerless through the efforts of the gods. And, ever since that time, by the power of Bhṛgu's curse, the Lord Viṣṇu is born again and again, when dharma is endangered, for the establishment of righteousness and the destruction of the demons.

CYAVANA (= C)
(*Mbh* III.121–24)

(121.22) Yudhiṣṭhira said:

1. Why was that great Bhārgava ascetic angry? How did he paralyze the blessed Pākaśāsana [Indra]?
2. And how, O brahman, did he make the Nāsatyas [Aśvins] drinkers of soma? May the blessed one tell me all this, just as it happened.

(122.1–27) Lomaśa said:

3. The great sage Bhṛgu had a son, a Bhārgava named Cyavana. This man of great splendor was once performing penances near a lake.
4. Adopting the "heroic posture" (*vīrasthāna*), O king, he stood motionless for a long time in one spot.
5. After a long time the wise man was built into a pile by ants and covered with creepers and he became to all appearances an anthill.
6. Thus closed in on every side, just like a lump of clay, the wise sage carried on his penances covered over by the anthill.[1]

[1] This immobility is characteristic of Cyavana. Cf. *Mbh* XIII.50, where he is covered with barnacles and seaweed. The anthill motif, of course, is better known in connection with the sage Vālmīki, legendary author of the *Rāmāyaṇa*. See *Adhyātma Rām.* Ayodhyākāṇḍa 6.42–88 and R. Goldman, "Vālmīki and the Bhṛgu Connection, *JAOS* 96, no. 1 (1976), 97–101.

7. After a long time, a king by the name of Śaryāti came to that charming and excellent lake for diversion.
8. His attendant women numbered four thousand.[2] One of them, O Bhārata, was his lovely daughter named Sukanyā.
9. While wandering about, attended by her female companions and adorned with every ornament, she came upon the Bhārgava's anthill.
10. Surrounded by her female companions, the pretty girl amused herself by gazing at the beautiful trees.
11. In her youth, beauty, playfulness, and passion, she broke off the thickly blossomed branches of the forest trees.
12. The wise Bhārgava saw her, alone, apart from her friends, wearing a single garment, and ornamented as she darted about like lightning.
13. The glorious sage was delighted to see her there in that deserted spot. The brahmanical seer, whose voice was feeble[3] through the practice of austerities, addressed the lovely girl, but she didn't hear him.

14–15. Then Sukanyā, seeing the Bhārgava's eyes in the anthill and impelled by her foolishness said, "What

[2] Notice how the situation of the characters, particularly that of the king, changes with the different contexts in which the episode occurs. The Śaryāta of the *ŚBr* appears to be a tribal ruler of the vedic age who moves about with his people (*grāma*, *ŚBr* IV.1.5.2). The Śaryāti of the *Mbh* is more closely approximate to the classical notion of a king, accompanied now, it appears, on an excursion by a large retinue and an armed force. Still, the notion of the royal outing is somewhat forced. The stereotyped epic device for getting a king into contact with a forest-dwelling sage is the hunting expedition. This, however, would not explain the crucial presence of Sukanyā. Hence, through the attempt to retain the situation more or less as it appears in the Brāhmaṇas, while still updating the sociological content, the *Mbh* presents the slightly bizarre picture of the king out for a day in the country, taking along four thousand women and an army as well.

[3] *kṣāmakaṇṭha*: lit. having a parched throat.

is this?" And she pierced his eyes with a thorn out of curiosity. When she had pierced his eye, the wrathful sage was furious. He blocked the passage of urine and feces by Śaryāti's army.

16. Then, when their urine and feces had been blocked the army was extremely discomfited by constipation. The king, when he saw his army in such a state, questioned them.
17. "Who here has this day injured the great and aged Bhārgava, who is constantly engaged in austerity and especially wrathful? Tell me at once this act of disrespect, whether it was intentional or unintentional."
18. The soldiers told him, "None of us knows what the injury was. But please, sire, use every possible means to find out."
19. Then the king interrogated his people first with gentle and then with harsh methods. But they didn't know.
20. But Sukanyā, seeing the army afflicted with constipation and misery, and her father unhappy, said this.
21. "While wandering about here, I saw a creature, which I took to be a firefly, shining in an anthill and I pierced it from close by."
22. When he heard that Śaryāti ran at once to the anthill. There he saw the Bhārgava, advanced both in years and in austerity.
23. The king, his hands folded humbly, pleaded for the sake of his army, "Please excuse that which was done to you in ignorance by a girl."

24–25. Then Cyavana the Bhārgava addressed the king. "I will be propitiated when I have taken your daughter, O king, that extremely beautiful girl who is a prey to greed and foolishness. This is the truth I tell you, king."

26. Saryāti agreed to the seer's words without hesitation and he gave his daughter to the great Cyavana.
27. Upon obtaining the maiden, Cyavana was propitiated. When the king had achieved that propitiation, he and his army moved on again.
28. As for the blameless Sukanyā, she, having obtained an ascetic husband, attended upon him constantly with affection, austerity, and devotion.
29. Free from malice and attentive to guests and the sacred fires, the lovely girl quickly pleased Cyavana.[4]

(123.1–23) Lomaśa said:

30. One day the Aśvins of the gods[5] saw Sukanyā naked after her bath.
31. The Aśvins or Nāsatyas, when they saw her whose body was as beautiful as that of the daughter of the king of the gods, came up to her and said:
32. "To whom do you belong, O girl of lovely thighs? What are you doing in the woods? We wish to know you, lovely one. Tell us the truth."
33. Then Sukanyā, when she was dressed, spoke to those two excellent gods. "Know that I am the daughter of Śaryāti and the wife of Cyavana."

[4] Sukanyā, it is to be noted, proves to be, unlike Reṇukā, the very model of fidelity.

[5] The meaning of the phrase *surāṇām aśvinau* is not clear to me. It would appear that the phrase seeks to draw a distinction between the Aśvins and the true gods. (The reading is marked as uncertain in the Crit. ed.) This would be in accord with their exclusion from the soma sacrifice. On the other hand the Aśvins as divinities are well known from the *RV* onwards without any indication of such a distinction. Moreover, at v. 4 they are themselves called *surottamau*. The issue is made explicit at vv. 61–64.

34. Laughing, the Asvins spoke to her again. "How is it, you lovely girl, that your father has given you to a decrepit man?[6]
35. You shine in the midst of the woods like forked lightning. We have not seen your like even among the gods.
36. You, a woman with a flawless body, should be enhanced, wearing the finest garments and adorned with every ornament, not covered like this with mud and filth.
37. Why, lovely lady, having come to such a condition, do you continue to serve a husband who is doddering with age and who is beyond the pleasures of sex,
38. a husband who is incapable of either protecting or supporting you? Enough! Leave Cyavana and choose one of us. You, who look like a daughter of the gods, should not waste your youth on your husband."
39. When they had spoken to her thus, Sukanyā said this to the two gods: "I am devoted to Cyavana. You should have no doubts in this matter."
40. The two celestial physicians spoke to her again. "We will make your husband young and handsome.
41. Then, calling out to one, you choose one husband, him or one of us."
42. After speaking with them she returned to the son of of Bhṛgu. She told him what they had said.
43. When he heard that, Cyavana said to his wife, "Let it be done!" As her husband agreed, she also said, "Let it be done!"

[6] *gatādhvan*: lit. "one who has traveled his road." Perhaps the English colloquialism "over the hill" best expresses the sense.

44. And when the Aśvins heard the princess say "Let it be done!" they told her "Let your husband enter the water."
45. Then, desiring beauty, Cyavana entered the water immediately. The Aśvins, too, entered that lake, O lord.
46. Then a moment later, they all emerged from the lake young, with heavenly beauty, wearing bright earrings, identical in form and inspiring love.
47. They all spoke at once, "Lovely lady, you of fair complexion, choose the one of us you desire to be your husband. Pick the one you desire, O lovely one."
48. The lady examined them as they stood there, identical in form, and, having reached a conclusion with her mind and heart[7] she picked her own husband.
49. When the powerful Cyavana had obtained his wife and the age and beauty that he desired, he was delighted and said these words to the Nāsatyas:

50–51. "Since you have made me, who was old, young and beautiful, and since I have obtained this wife, I will, out of affection, make you two drinkers of soma right before the eyes of the king of the gods. This that I tell you is the truth."

[7] The Crit. ed. does not indicate exactly how Sukanyā is able to distinguish her husband from the Aśvins. Some MSS add two more verses to the effect that she resorts to a truth-act based upon her constant devotion to her husband. The appeal is made directly to the Aśvins and they give her her husband. See the critical apparatus to v. 19 in the Crit. ed. for the verses. The episode is reminiscent of Damayantī's correct identification of Nala from among the gods who had taken his form at *Mbh* III.54.10–25. In the Nala story, however, the basis for Damayantī's discrimination is made clear.

52. Hearing that, those two were delighted and went back to heaven. But Cyavana and Sukanyā engaged in lovemaking like a couple of celestials.

(124.1–24) Lomaśa said:

53. Śaryāti was delighted when he heard that Cyavana was restored to youth, and so he came to the Bhārgava's ashram with his army.
54. Upon seeing Cyavana and Sukanyā, who looked like children of the gods, Śaryāti, protector of the earth, was as pleased as if he had obtained the whole earth.
55. That lord of the earth was hospitably received by the sage and, seated nearby, the great-minded one engaged him in pleasant conversation.
56. Then, O king, the Bhārgava, by way of conciliation, said to him, "I will sacrifice for you, king. See to the necessary preparations."
57. Śaryāti, lord of the earth, was greatly pleased, and respectfully heeded Cyavana's speech, O great king.
58. On an auspicious day, the one appointed for the sacrifice, Śaryāti had a sacrificial ground laid out conducive to the fulfillment of all desires.
59. There, O king, the Bhārgava Cyavana sacrificed for him. Now learn from me the extraordinary things that took place there.
60. Cyavana took up the soma for the twin gods, the Aśvins. Then Indra stopped him as he was taking up their ladle.
61. Indra said:

    "It is my opinion that these two Nāsatyas are not worthy of soma. These physicians are not deserving of the sacrifice of the sons of the gods."

62. Cyavana said:
"Maghavan, do not despise these two great beings, greatly endowed with wealth and beauty, who have made me as ageless as a god.

63. How is it that, unlike you and the other gods, these two are not worthy of soma? Know, O chief of the gods, that the Aśvins too are gods."

64. Indra said:
"How can these two, who are physicians and servants, who take on any shape at will,[8] and who move about in the world of mortals, be worthy of soma here?"

65. Lomaśa said:
Then while Vāsava went on repeating these words, the Bhārgava, ignoring him, took up the ladle.

66. Balabhid [Indra], seeing him about to ladle out the excellent soma for the Aśvins, spoke these words:

67. "If you take up the soma for these two, I will hurl upon you the unequaled thunderbolt weapon (*vajra*), of terrifying form."

68. When he had been addressed in this way, the Bhārgava, smiling and looking at Indra, offered the soma and an excellent ladle to the Aśvins in the proper fashion.

69. Then Śacipati [Indra] started to hurl the dreadful thunderbolt at him. But the Bhārgava paralyzed his arm as he was throwing it.

70. When he had paralyzed him the very powerful Cyavana recited mantras and made offerings to the

[8] Indra's objection that the Aśvins are *kāmarūpasamanvitau* is, to say the least, hypocritical. See *Mbh* XIII.40.28–38 for an elaborate description of his own shape-changing.

fire for the sake of [producing] an evil spirit, and intent on destroying the god.

71. Thence arose an evil spirit through the power of the sage's austerity: the great asura of great power and huge form, called Mada [Intoxication], [the extent of] whose body the gods and the demons were unable to fathom.

72. His mouth was huge and terrible, with sharp teeth. One of his jaws rested on the earth, the other reached the sky.

73. He had four fangs, each a thousand leagues[9] in extent. His other teeth were ten leagues high and looked like a palisade of spear points.

74. His arms were equal, ten thousand leagues in length, and looked like mountains. His eyes resembled the sun and moon, and his mouth looked like death.

75–76. This creature of terrible demeanor, licking his chops with a tongue lolling like darting lightning, his jaws gaping as if to swallow forcibly the whole world, ran in a fury at Śatakratu [Indra] to eat him. While running so he made the worlds resound with a great and terrible sound.

(125.1–10) 77. Lomaśa said:
The god Śatakratu saw Mada with his terrible face, coming like death about to eat [him] with gaping jaws.

78. The king of the gods, his arm paralyzed, licked the corners of his mouth repeatedly in fear. Oppressed with fear he spoke to Cyavana.

[9] *yojana*: a unit of distance for which varying values are given. It is however generally said to measure four *krośas* or approximately nine miles. It is thus technically much longer than an English league.

79. "The Aśvins shall be worthy of soma from now on, O Bhārgava. I am telling you the truth, O brahman.
80. No undertaking of yours is in vain. Let this be the supreme rule. I know, brahman-sage, that nothing you do is in vain.
81. These Aśvins are worthy of soma, for you have made them so today. May your power be made manifest again, Bhārgava.
82. May the fame of Sukanyā's father spread throughout the world. Be gracious to me, since what I did served to show your power. Let this be as you wish."
83. When he was thus addressed by Śakra, the great Cyavana's anger quickly vanished and he released Purandara [Indra].
84. The mighty man apportioned Mada, whom he had created, among strong drink, women, dice, and hunting.
85. When he had thus disposed of Mada, and satisfied Śakra and the gods including the Aśvins by means of soma, he sacrificed for the king.
86. Having made known his power in all the worlds, that foremost of eloquent men sported in the woods with his beloved Sukanyā.

ŚUKRA AND ŚIVA (= ŚŚ)
(*Mbh* XII.278.1–38)

Yudhiṣṭhira said:

1. Father, this curiosity is always in my heart. I wish to hear this from you, grandfather of the Kurus:
2. How did the divine sage Uśanas Kāvya, a man of great intellect, become a constant benefactor of the asuras, dedicated to injuring the gods?
3. Why did he increase the power of those whose power is measureless?[1] Why are the dānavas forever locked in enmity with the gods?
4. How did Uśanas of divine splendor become Śukra? How did he attain greatness? Tell me all of this.
5. How is it that that powerful one does not travel

[1] *vardhayām āsa tejaś ca kimartham amitaujasām*: like much of this passage, this half verse is less than perfectly clear. The last word is marked as an uncertain reading in the critical edition. A number of MSS read *amitadyutiḥ*, "man of measureless splendor." This would refer to Śukra and the question would then concern the way in which he augmented his own power. Nīl. perhaps idiosyncratically glosses *vardhayāmāsa* as *ciccheda*, "cut off," "destroyed." He takes *amitaujasām* to refer to the gods. Its apparent reference, however, is to the asuras.

through the air? Grandfather, I want to know that in its entirety.

Bhīṣma said:

6. Blameless king, listen attentively to this whole story, according to my understanding, that I heard long ago.
7. This descendant of the Bhārgavas, a perfected sage, firm in his vows, was well disposed toward the asuras because of compassion.[2]
8. Now lord[3] Dhanada [Kubera] is a king, the ruler of the yakṣas and the rakṣases. He is lord of treasure and lord of the world.
9. The great sage, perfect in yoga entered [Dhanada's] body and, having immobilized the god, lord of wealth, he stole his riches by means of yoga.
10. When Dhanada's wealth had been stolen he took no

[2] *karuṇātmake*: the word is marked with a wavy line in the Crit. ed. as uncertain. Variants are *karaṇā* and *kāraṇā*. Nīl., commenting on the latter, takes *kāraṇa* to equal *kriyā*. The action or cause referred to, he says, is the slaying of Kāvya's mother by Viṣṇu, an abbreviated account of which Nīl. gives. It is similar to the story related at length at *MatsyaP* 47 and *PadmaP* 5.13.202 ff., but here Nīl. traces Kāvya's association with the asuras to this event, whereas in the purāṇic account, the event comes about as a consequence of that association.

[3] *indraḥ*: There is some confusion here as to the reference of this word. Is it a proper noun, or is it simply an adjective modifying *dhanada*? Both interpretations have been offered. Nīl. understands the verse to refer to two figures, Indra and Kubera. Thus he takes the word *prabhuḥ* to refer distributively to both of them: *indro jagataḥ prabhur dhanadas tadīyakośasya prabhur ity anvayaḥ*, "Indra is the lord of the world and Dhanada of its treasure. That is the construction." On the other hand, there is no further reference to Indra in this verse or in any of the following verses. In fact, the king of the gods has nothing whatever to do with this story. Because of this, I am inclined to agree with the commentator Arjunamiśra in his explanation: "*indra* is an adjective modifying *dhanada*."

The identification of Kubera as lord not only of the yakṣas but also of the rakṣases is to be noted.

pleasure in anything. Agitated, his spirit dejected, he approached the greatest of the gods [Śiva].

11. He reported to Śiva, to Rudra of measureless power, the greatest of the gods, the beneficent, bearer of many forms.

Kubera said:

12. "Uśanas, whose essence is yoga, immobilized me and stole my riches. And making his own way[4] by means of yoga he escaped."

13. Then, O king, when the great yogi Maheśvara [Śiva] heard that he was furious. His eyes red [with anger], he seized his trident and stood.

14. Having taken up that supreme weapon he said, "Where is he? Where is he?" Knowing his intention from afar, Uśanas appeared.

15. Aware of the great yogi's [Śiva's] anger, the lord [Śukra] knew his coming, going, and position.[5]

16. Concentrating with great ascetic power on the great Maheśvara, Uśanas, whose mind was perfected in yoga, appeared on the point of his trident.

17. The bowman [Śiva], perfect in austerity, made out his form, and recognizing him, the lord of the gods bent the trident with his hand.

[4] *ātmagatim*: usually "one's own way or course" evidently a reference to Śukra's complete mastery over the lord of wealth. The idea is that he can come and go as he pleases or that he makes his own path. The commentator Vidyāsāgara, however, takes the term as a reference to the pores and other openings of Kubera's body that serve as the means of the clever Bhārgava's access to and egress from the body [*ātman*] of his victim: *niḥsaraṇamārgam romakūpādikam*.

[5] *gatim āgamanaṃ vetti sthānaṃ vetti*: I understand this in a general sense. Śukra, through his yogic and supernatural perception, is fully aware of Śiva's movements. As with several other points this strange battle of master yogins, the exact meaning is arguable.

18. Then, since he had bent the trident with his hand, the lord whose weapons are terrible and whose power is measureless called the trident *pināka*.[6]
19. Kākudin [Śiva], the husband of Umā, seeing the Bhārgava standing in his hand, opened his mouth and slowly put his hand in it.
20. But the lord Uśanas, great scion of Bhṛgu's race, having entered Maheśvara's belly, moved about[7] there.

Yudhiṣṭhira said:

21. Why did Uśanas move about in the stomach of the wise god of gods? What else did that man of great splendor do?

Bhīṣma said:

22. First, having entered the waters, he whose vows were great[8] [Śukra] became immobile. Millions and tens of millions of years went by, O king.

[6] This, too, is a problematic verse. The syntax of the four instrumentals in the first half is far from clear. The commentator Vādirāja suggests that the last two be taken as locatives (*amitatejasā pāninā iti tṛtīyā saptamyarthe*). I have followed his advice and take the phrase as a locative absolute. Nīl. provides an explanation of this apparent etymology. See note 34 chapter 3.

[7] *vyacarat*: Nil. remarks that the sage was not digested like food and that it should be added that he performed austerities in the god's stomach. This last remark is in keeping with Nīl's understanding of the whole episode, an understanding which is on the whole correct.

[8] *mahāvrataḥ*: v. 22 and the four that follow it constitute the core of the struggle between Śukra and Śiva. Unfortunately these verses are the most obscure of an already difficult passage, largely because the epithets used for the two rivals are frequently ambiguous, so that, at crucial junctures, it is difficult to ascertain just who is being spoken of. This confusion is further intensified by the introduction, in v. 23, of Brahman, who functions in an obscure capacity. Moreover, the text seems somewhat corrupt here and may have been unclear to redactors and/or scribes of the available manuscript traditions.

First, who is the "one of great vows" who enters the waters to perform great and difficult austerities? Is the god seeking to master the sage, or is Śukra at-

23. Having performed difficult austerity, he came up out of the great pool. Then Brahman, the supreme lord of the gods, approached him.[9]

24. He asked him about the increase in his [Śukra's?][10] austerities, his prosperity, and his well-being. He

---

tempting to brazen out his predicament? Is Śiva in the ocean, or are the waters in the god's stomach? Belvalkar, in his critical notes to the passage, understands Śiva to be the practitioner of the submarine penances. In support of this interpretation he cites *Mbh.* X.17.11 in which Harikeśa (Śiva) performs austerities for a long time while immersed in the waters. Then, too, the adjective *sthāṇubhūta*, "having become immobile," suggests the widely used epithet of Śiva, Sthāṇu. On the other hand, underwater austerity is a feat accomplished at least twice by Bhārgava sages. Cyavana is said to have performed such an act at the confluence of the Ganges and Yamunā rivers (*Mbh* XIII.50.4 ff.), and in doing so is said to have become *sthāṇubhūta* (ibid., v. 6). Moreover, Śukra himself in the *PadmaP* variant of ŚA, making an unequivocal reference to this episode, states: *nanu śiṣyabhayād yātaḥ pūrvam evam ahaṃ vibho/jalamadhyasthitaḥ pīto mahādevena śambhunā//*(*PadmaP* V.13.303) "Indeed, lord, long ago when I had gone off in this way because of danger to my disciples, and was in the midst of the water, I was drunk up by Mahādeva Śambhu." Aside from this there are textual and contextual issues that bear, sometimes in opposite directions, on the question. The critical text of vv. 23–24 does seem to indicate Śiva as the practitioner of the austerities, although the matter is far from clear. On the other hand, several narrative and contextual issues would appear to override the shaky evidence of these verses. These questions will be examined in detail in the succeeding notes.

[9] *Brahman*: This verse is somewhat confusing. According to the critical text Brahman approaches someone, most probably Śiva. One MS used for the Crit. ed. attempts to reverse this with the reading *brahmāṇam upasarpata*, "He [the supreme lord of the gods, now Śiva] approached Brahman." The problem becomes even more complex in the next verse.

[10] *tapovṛddhim apṛcchac ca . . .*: v. 24 is critical, and presents several thorny problems. The first concerns the point of Brahman's questions. Is he asking Śiva about that god's own austerity and well being; or is he asking about the progress of the swallowed sage? On first thought the former would seem likely, since the words are part of the usual greeting formalities well known to epic poetry (cf. *Rām.* I.17.29). Indeed Śiva's reply seems quite in keeping with this interpretation. Yet in vv. 25 and 26 it is stated, first, that someone perceived this increase (*vṛddhi*) in the power of austerity by virtue of some special contact (*tatsaṃyoga*) and that second, as a result of these austerities someone was enriched and became eminent

whose emblem is the bull [Śiva] replied that his austerities were well observed.

25. The wise Śaṅkara [Śiva] whose essence is inconceivable and who is ever devoted to truth and dharma perceived the increase through contact with him [Śukra].
26. The powerful great yogi [Śukra] was enriched by that [austerity] in wealth and ascetic power, O king. He became eminent in the three worlds.
27. Then Pinākin [Śiva], whose essence is yoga, entered into profound meditation[11]. Uśanas was terrified and hid[12] in his stomach.
28. Even where he was the great yogi praised the god. Desiring to escape he was prevented by [blazing] power.

---

in the three worlds. Now surely the great god needs no special contact to perceive the progress of his own mortifications. Moreover it seems hardly appropriate to state that the lord of the universe became enriched or eminent. These considerations make it more than likely that Nīl. is correct in taking *tapovṛddhi* to refer to Śukra's increase in power and in viewing the Bhārgava as the great yogi of v. 26. Nīl. takes *tatsaṃyogena* to mean *tapoyogena*, "through the application of the power of austerity." In this light it seems likely but nonetheless surprising that Brahman is asking Śiva about Śukra's progress and that Śiva by virtue of having the sage in his own belly is able to answer his questions. *vṛṣabhadhvajaḥ*: The nominative case-ending of this common epithet for Śiva is marked in the critical text as uncertain. Some eleven MSS collated for the Crit. ed. show the accusative *vṛsabhadhvajam*. Should this reading be accepted, it would accord with the reversal of the roles between Śiva and Brahmā suggested by the variant given in footnote 9 above.

[11] *dhyānayogam*: This marks the beginning of Śiva's meditation which counters and outmatches Śukra's austerities.

[12] *nililye*: The usual meanings of *nilī* are to cling fast and to hide. Nīl., however, takes the perfect *nililye* as meaning *nitarām babhrāma*. Thus he feels that Śukra is moving about. This verse, with its information that only now, having understood the situation, does Śiva resort to yogic meditation to rid himself of his troublesome guest, confirms the view that the previous description of trance and penance refer to the activities of the Bhārgava sage.

29. Then, O subduer of your foes, the great sage Uśanas, remaining in his [Śiva's] belly, said over and over again, "Be gracious to me."
30. Mahādeva, bull among the gods, closed all his bodily openings and said to him, "Get your freedom through my penis."
31. Closed in on all sides, not seeing an opening, the sage went this way and that being burned by the [blazing] power.
32. Coming out through his penis he became Śukra [semen]. Because of that action he did not travel through the air.
33. Then seeing him who had come out blazing, as it were, from his power, Bhava [Śiva] was suffused with anger and stood with his trident raised.
34. Devī stopped Paśupati [Śiva], her angry husband. When Śaṅkara was checked, [Śukra] became Devī's son.

Devī said:

35. "You should not harm him who has become my son. For no one who has come forth from the belly of a god may perish."

Bhīṣma said:

36. Then, O king, pacified by Devī and smiling he [Śiva] said over and over again, "Let him go as he likes."
37. Then having done homage to the boon-granting god and also to the goddess Umā, that great sage, the wise Uśanas, attained the state that he had desired.
38. My boy, I have related to you the deeds of the great Bhārgava about which you asked me, O best of the descendants of Bharata.

CYAVANA AND KUŚIKA (=CK) (*Mbh* XIII.52.1–9; 55.9–12, 27–35; 56.1–20)

Yudhiṣṭhira said:

1. Wise one, I have a doubt as large as the ocean. Hear it from me, O great-armed one, and having heard it, please clarify it.
2. Lord, I have the greatest curiosity with regard to Rāma Jāmadagnya, the greatest of the upholders of dharma. Please clarify this for me.
3. How was it that Rāma was born as one of true valor? How was one of kṣatriya practices born in a line of brahman sages?
4. Tell me about his origin in detail, O king. Also how did a brahman come from the Kauśikas, a kṣatriya family?
5. Ah! The enormous power of those two great ones, Rāma and Viśvāmitra, O tiger among men!
6. How did this irregularity[1] skip over the sons and

[1] *doṣa*: This is the only passage in the epic which explicitly refers to the role switch as a flaw or irregularity. In the other versions this is implicit in Satyavatī's horror at the idea.

leaving them [unaffected] then manifest itself in the grandsons? Please explain this to me.

Bhīṣma said:

7. Regarding this, O Bhārata, they recount this ancient legend [called] "The conversation between Cyavana and Kuśika."

8–9. Having long ago foreseen this future irregularity in his own line, and having weighed in his mind all its advantages and disadvantages, its strengths and weaknesses, Cyavana, a Bhārgava ascetic, a man of great intelligence and a bull among sages, desired to burn up the family of the Kauśikas.

[*After an elaborate but unsuccessful attempt to provoke king Kuśika, Cyavana is pacified and reconciled to the future exchange of class-roles. Then, in response to the king's questions the sage explains the motive for his provocation.*]

(55.9–12) Cyavana said:

10. Now hear it all without omission, what this was and for what reason. For when I am questioned in this way, O king, I must explain.

11. Hear from me, O king, as I relate it, what I heard long ago, in the assembly of the gods while Pitāmaha [Brahman] was speaking.

12. Through the hostility between the brahmans and the kṣatriyas a mixing of the races[2] will occur. Your grandson, O king, will be endowed with spiritual power and physical might.

[2] *kulasaṃkara*: This is the only Bhārgava passage which calls attention to the Bhṛgus' prediliction for marrying the daughters of kṣatriyas. It is certainly the only one which condemns the practice as miscegenation. Cyavana does not make clear how this miscegenation is to be the result of hostility.

13. Therefore I came to you, for the protection of my own race, wishing to burn up yours, wishing to bring about the end of the Kuśikas.

(55.27c–36) 14. Your wish in this affair is also known to me, O king.

15. Disdaining the lordship of men and lordship of the gods, you desire brahmanhood and austerity, O king, lord of the earth.

16. It is just as you said, my son: brahmanhood is hard to attain. Even if brahmanhood is attained, the status of a seer (*ṛṣi*) is hard to attain. Even if the status of a seer is attained, the status of an ascetic (*tapasvin*) is hard to attain.

17–19. This desire of yours will be fulfilled: there will be a Kauśika brahman from the Kauśika family. O best of kings, your family will attain brahmanhood in the third generation through the power of the Bhṛgus. Your grandson will be an ascetic priest[3] with the splendor of fire who will inspire fear in men, gods, and the three worlds. This that I tell you is the truth.

20. Take this boon that is in your mind, O royal seer. Time is passing. I will soon go on a pilgrimage.

Kuśika said:

21. Let this be my boon this day if it please you, great sage. Let this be as you said, blameless one: ascetic power for my grandson. Let my family have brahmanhood, O blessed one. This is my boon.

22. In addition, blessed one, I wish you to explain at

[3] *vipra*: The critical edition has with uncertainty accepted the vocative *vipra*, "O priest." This seems inappropriate as a mode of address for the king Kuśika, to whose family priesthood is not to come for two more generations. I have therefore accepted the variant *vipraḥ*, the nominative, which occurs in several of the MSS collated by the critical edition.

length: how will my family attain brahmanhood, O scion of the Bhṛgus? Who will this kinsman of mine be? Who will be renowned?

(56.1–20) Cyavana said:

23. Bull among men! Lord of the sons of Manu! I must surely tell you that on account of which I came to bring about your end.

24. Lord of the people! The kṣatriyas are the constant patrons of the Bhṛgus; but, for a fated reason [the two groups] will come to quarrel.

25. The kṣatriyas, O lord of men, afflicated by the rod of fate, will kill all the Bhṛgus, slaughtering them down to the unborn embryos.

26. Then in our race will be born a perpetuator of his line named Aurva, a man of great power, equal in splendor to the blazing sun.

27. He will generate a fire of wrath to destroy the triple world that will reduce the earth, along with its mountains and forests, to ashes.[4]

28. But after some time that best of sages will himself extinguish the fire, having cast it into the "mare's mouth"[5] in the sea.

29. O sinless one, the entire dhanurveda will be directly revealed to his illustrious son Ṛcīka, a scion of the Bhṛgus.

30–31. And he, having mastered it for the destruction of the kṣatriyas, will, for a fated reason, pass it on to his son, the illustrious Jamadagni, whose mind will be

[4] The destruction of the earth is not known to the Aurva episode of the epic.

[5] *vaḍavāvaktre*: The submarine cave whence the underwater fire emanates. Cf. A 58.

purified through austerity. And this tiger of the Bhṛgus too [Jamadagni] will preserve that veda.

32. And, O righteous one, he will take a girl from your family[6] for the exaltation of your family, O best of kings.

33. That man of great ascetic power will take Gādhi's daughter, your granddaughter, and will father Rāma, a brahman of kṣatriya practices.

34. O man of great splendor, he will give to your family a kṣatriya of brahmanical deeds, Viśvāmitra, the righteous son of Gādhi endowed with great ascetic power, the equal of Bṛhaspati in might.

35. By the command of Pitāmaha two women[7] will cause this reversal. This will not come about otherwise.

36. Brahmanhood will come to you in the third generation. You will be a kinsman of the pure-minded Bhṛgus.

Bhīsma said:

37. Then, O best of Bhāratas, when the righteous king Kuśika had heard the words of the great sage Cyavana, he was delighted and said these words: "So be it."

38. Then Cyavana, whose power was great, once more urged that best of men to ask a boon. The king said to him,

39. "Very well. I will accept a boon from you, great sage. May my line become brahmanical and may its mind be on dharma."

40. When he had been addressed in this way the sage

[6] Note the confusion of Jamadagni with Ṛcīka.

[7] Satyavatī and her mother.

replied, "So be it." Then taking his leave of the king, he went on a pilgrimage.

41. O king, I have told you all about the cause of the connection of the Bhṛgus and the Kauśikas, omitting nothing.
42. Everything, O king, the births of Rāma and of the sage Viśvāmitra, took place as the sage had said.

Part 2
Myth and Metamyth

1
Masters of Life and Death

The themes of life and death are essential to any great literature, and Sanskrit literature is no exception. The *Mahābhārata* is especially concerned with such matters. It is in part a treatise on these themes, instructing men how to live and die in accordance with a social, moral, and spiritual order. Yet even in this massive epic, with its countless battles, murders, genocidal vendettas, and religious suicides, the myths of the Bhārgava cycle stand out for their concern with death, especially violent death, in its various forms.

Non-Bhārgava brahmans are subjected to violent death only sporadically in the epic.[1] In contrast, the Bhṛgu sages are slain or threatened with violence in almost every major myth of the cycle,[2] and their wives, mothers, and even unborn children are also subject to this pervasive violence. In one important instance the entire Bhṛgu race is said to have been slaughtered. A number of myths seem even to indicate a sort of death-wish or suicidal undercurrent to the cycle. The theme is frequently inverted, and Bhārgava sages themselves often attack and kill their enemies, not sparing the unborn. In one case a Bhṛgu even kills his own mother.

In addition to being especially distinguished as the victims and agents of violent death, the Bhṛgus are also set apart as the special repositories of the power to revive the dead. This power and its exercise constitute one of the most striking and characteristic features of the Bhārgava cycle.

The two themes are closely related in the minds and the myths of the Bhṛgus, and in many cases the Bhārgavas who are killed are subsequently restored to life.

The Bhṛgus as Victims

In a cycle of myths whose general thrust is the glorification of the Bhṛgus, no theme is as initially perplexing as that of the Bhṛgus as murder victims. Nonetheless, its frequency and elaborateness demonstrate clearly that the theme had a firm hold on the minds of the mythmakers and served an important function in their tradition.

In various versions of the epic Bhārgava myths, the important Bhṛgus Jamadagni and Śukra are said to have died violent deaths (R 49–50, ŚK 49). In the myth of Aurva the entire clan is put to death (A 8). Śukra is threatened with murderous violence by Śiva (ŚŚ 13), as is Cyavana by Indra (C 67). Wives of prominent Bhṛgus are twice murdered. Jamadagni's wife Reṇukā is slain by her own son (R 38), and the wife of Bhṛgu himself is killed by Viṣṇu (ŚA 43). In many cases the actual circumstances of these deaths and death threats are so similar as to preclude coincidence.

The events of the Aurvopākhyāna (A) are especially dramatic. They are also perplexing. The genocidal fury of the descendants of the king Kṛtavīrya seems out of proportion to the provocation, while the switch from amity to hostility between the two clans is puzzling (A 7–8). Yet of all the peculiar features of this episode none is so startling as the extraordinary statement of the *pitṛs*, the spirits of the dead Bhṛgus, that they themselves deliberately provoked their own massacre (A 30–34).

If, as the cyclic nature of the Bhārgava mythology suggests, themes and motifs are subject to a high degree of borrowing and rearrangement, it is appropriate to examine the function and the integration of such elements in their various contexts. The motif of racial death-wish on the part of the Bhṛgus in the Aurvopākhyāna is interesting in this regard. Its function is clear: it is related to the whole question of the Bhārgava provenance of the epic. The issue is the Bhṛguid redactors' assertion of power and supremacy on behalf of their clan. As Sukthankar remarked, "How could those puny Kṣatriyas ever hope to kill the Bhārgavas? That *contretemps* was a little contrivance of the Bhārgavas themselves."[3] The motif preserves the initiative and dignity of the Bhṛgus.

The transparency of the motif-function raises other, more complex questions concerning the source of this strange episode. A notable lack of integration of the motif into the narrative development of the Aurva myth would seem to suggest that it is an interpolation. The motif is introduced abruptly, without any prior intimation of such a highly charged notion as racial suicide.[4] Moreover, the statement of the Bhārgava pitṛs concerning their motivation accords poorly with an earlier portion of the narrative in which the Bhṛgus variously concealed their wealth, gave it to other brahmans, or gave it to the kṣatriyas (A 5–6). Presumably those who acceded to the warriors' demands did so to avoid antagonizing them. Most striking of all is the fact that the bizarre and elaborate explanation appears to make no impression whatever upon Aurva. Ignoring the argument of the pitṛs, he persists in his wrath and rails against the fact that the Bhṛgus, when attacked by the warriors, could find no one to protect them (A 42–48). One would expect that if the motif were original to the Aurvopākhyāna it would not present these difficulties. Since it does not advance the plot in any way, nor function in its own right as an important structural element, it appears likely that it was interpolated to salvage Bhārgava prestige or for other reasons.

There is some evidence that the motif of racial suicide is known elsewhere in Bhārgava myth.[5] However, in this case it appears that the motif, like the Aurva episode as a whole, may have been heavily influenced by another cycle of myths with which it is intimately associated, the cycle concerning the sage Vasiṣṭha.[6]

The sage Jamadagni is the only other Bhārgava to be killed by kṣatriyas,[7] and the story of his death (see R) is of particular interest for its evident relation to the Aurva episode.[8] Jamadagni, like the Bhṛgus of the Aurva myth, is killed by kṣatriyas of the Haihaya clan, the descendants of the king Kṛtavīrya (A 1–3, R 50–51).[9] The Aurva story speaks of the king Kṛtavīrya as being a friend and patron of the Bhṛgus (A 1–2). In the story of Jamadagni, the king is said to be the thousand-armed Arjuna Kārtavīrya (R 43). *Mahābhārata* versions of this story differ sharply as to his character and his behavior toward the Bhṛgus,[10] but in both myths it is the kings' descendants, not the kings themselves, who commit murder. In both cases the brahmans are killed with arrows (A 8, R 51,54–56). In neither episode do the victims make any attempt to defend themselves, although there is good reason to believe that they are fully capable of doing so.[11]

The episode of the murder of Jamadagni is also like the Aurvopākhyāna in that some of its major motifs are clearly derivative. The most obvious example concerns the incident that gives rise to the conflict resulting in the death of the sage.

Kārtavīrya's (or his sons') theft of Jamadagni's calf plays a vital role in the development of the episode, yet in the context of the story and of Bhṛguid mythology his action seems inexplicable. No epic version of the episode provides any explanation of why a prince would wish to steal a calf. Such an act would be explicable only if there were something especially valuable about the animal. In neither epic version is this said to be the case.[12] The motif of a prince abducting the cow of a forest-dwelling sage is, however, to be found greatly elaborated in the well-known episode of Viśvāmitra and the wish-fulfilling cow of Vasiṣṭha.[13] In that episode the action of the king is entirely plausible. Moreover, the wonderful wish-cow is regularly associated with Vasiṣṭha even in other contexts;[14] nowhere in the epic is she associated with the Bhṛgus.[15] Here, too, as in the Aurva myth, the motif is borrowed from one of the cycle of myths associated with the sage Vasiṣṭha and his family.[16]

The only other Bhārgava sage to be killed in the epic dies under unusual circumstances. Śukra is killed when, in order to escape from a seemingly insoluble dilemma, he summons his dead pupil Kaca to burst forth from his belly (ŚK 44–49). The episode is of greater interest in connection with the motif of the restoration of the dead, but it is worth noting here that this is one of the few Bhārgava myths in which allusion is made to *brahmahatyā*, the great sin of killing a brahman (ŚK 39,54).[17]

In two other Bhṛguid myths in the *Mahābhārata*, major Bhārgava sages are threatened with violence but manage to escape injury. In both cases the would-be assailants are gods. The first, the hostile encounter of Cyavana and Indra, is perhaps the oldest attested Bhārgava myth.[18] It exerts a fascination on the Bhārgava redactors second only to that of the myth of Rāma Jāmadagnya.[19] Indra attacks Cyavana with his terrible *vajra*, or thunderbolt, but is foiled by the sage (C 67–69). The god seems to show no initial fear of the sage or concern about the sin of slaying a brahman.[20] The second is yet another of the strange episodes involving Śukra. Here the great lord Śiva makes several attempts to destroy him without success (ŚŚ 14–20,33–34).

The theme of Bhārgavas suffering violent death has one further motif, the murder of the sages' wives. This motif, occuring twice[21] in the Sanskrit mythological literature, appears to be wholly restricted to the Bhārgava corpus, while the parallelism between the two occurrences is such that it can hardly be doubted that one is a transposition of the other. The women involved are Reṇukā, the wife of Jamadagni and mother of the Bhārgava Rāma, and an unnamed woman who is the wife of Bhṛgu and the mother of Śukra. Both women are beheaded (R 38; ŚA 43).[22]

The murder of Reṇukā is especially interesting in that it is done by her son Rāma at the command of her husband.[23] On the other hand, like the motif of racial suicide in the Aurva story, it seems to have little if any connection with the narrative context in which it occurs. The incident is introduced abruptly, in no way following from what precedes it, and its lack of continuity with what follows it is pronounced. The episode provides no contribution to the development of the narrative, since all its effects are immediately undone. Jamadagni's anger (R 33), his curse of his sons (R 36), the murder itself, and the sin incurred by the son are all immediately negated by Jamadagni's boon (R 40–42). The only positive results of the boon are the rather vague ones of long life and excellence in battle. Even Reṇukā's remembrance of the murder is effaced, and she appears immediately afterwards when the main narrative is resumed (R 43).[24] The remainder of the story and all its other versions in the epic make no allusion to this interlude.

With regard to narrative weight, the killing of Śukra's mother (see ŚA) contrasts sharply to the Reṇukā episode. Like

Reṇukā, she is restored to life by her husband (ŚA 47–52); but both her death and her resurrection serve definite narrative functions in the story and are well integrated with what follows them. Śukra's mother's conflict with Indra and Viṣṇu develops naturally out of the elaborate interplay among the gods, the demons, and Śukra that precedes it (ŚA 1–29). Moreover, Bhṛgu's dramatic revival of his wife serves to alarm Indra about the seemingly limitless power of the Bhārgava sages and sets in motion the action of the remainder of the extensive story (ŚA 53 ff.). In addition, the detail and elaboration of the episode is quite different from the peculiar terseness of the Reṇukā story, in which even extraordinary events, such as Rāma's killing of his mother and Jamadagni's restoration of the slain woman to life, are passed over with the merest mention. It is likely that the motif has been borrowed by the Rāma myth from the myth of Śukra, and it is evident that such manipulation of submythic elements is of significance in the generation of the Bhārgava cycle.

The Bhṛgus as Killers

Intimately associated with the motifs just discussed are a series of motifs in which the Bhṛgus are the purveyors of violence. In most cases one of the latter motifs is contiguous with one of the former, and the pairs thus formed generally constitute the myths of aggression and retaliation so favored by the Bhārgava mythmakers.

Although the theme of violence directed against brahmans is largely restricted to the Bhārgava cycle and mythic material with which it is often associated, the theme of the deadly anger of brahmans is to be found throughout the literature.[25] Its application to the Bhārgava cycle of myths, however, is unusual in several respects. In the first place, the incidence of such violence, actual or threatened, is particularly marked among the Bhṛgus. At least six of them, including the wife of Bhṛgu himself, kill or threaten to kill their enemies. Also, to a degree found in the myths of no other priestly clan,[26] the gods are the objects of Bhārgava violence. Most important of all is the fact that the most violent of the Bhārgavas, the only one who actually carries out a crusade of genocide, does so in a manner almost wholly alien to the brahmanical tradition.[27]

Four of the Bhṛgus threaten gods with death. Cyavana responds to Indra's attack (C 69) by creating a colossal monster which he looses on the terrified god (C 70–74).[28] It is only when Indra accedes to the sage's wishes and humbly begs his pardon that Cyavana decides to spare him (C 77–83). In an inversion of this sequence, Viṣṇu beheads Śukra's mother only when she is on the point of slaying both him and Indra (ŚA 34–43). Jamadagni, the victim of Kṛtavīrya's sons and the instigator of violence against his own wife, is elsewhere said to have threatened to shoot the sun-god Sūrya;[29] while in a passage that contains a number of variants of typically Bhārgava motifs, the young sage Vipula, incensed, drives Indra away after telling him that he will spare his life.[30]

The motif of vengeance withheld is most fully developed in the story of Aurva. There the infant sage sets his mind on nothing less than the destruction of the universe (A 24–27). The way in which he comes to this decision is no less interesting than the arguments by which his departed ancestors seek to dissuade him from it.

The desire to destroy the world is not Aurva's immediate reaction to the kṣatriyas' massacre of his clan. His anger is initially directed only against the offending warriors, whom he blinds with his splendor as soon as he is born (A 11). It is evident that the sage intends to destroy the princes in his anger at their crimes.[31] This reaction is natural and wholly in keeping with the traditions of brahmanical myth, both Bhārgava and non-Bhārgava. Yet Aurva's revenge is not carried out. The blinded descendants of Kṛtavīrya, acting on the advice of Aurva's mother, approach the furious child to ask forgiveness and he is instantly appeased (A 22). Thus far, the story, though peculiar, is logical. Then, however, after having been successfully propitiated, Aurva surprisingly decides to undertake a universal destruction of guilty and innocent alike (A 24–27).[32] It is from this apparently irrational plan that the Bhṛgu ancestors must dissuade Aurva with their own equally inconsistent arguments. Aurva's reasons for his proposed holocaust are themselves flawed for various reasons, not least among which is the universality of his plan.

Not only is his belated plan strange in the light of his prior release of the actual perpetrators of the massacre, but his desire to avenge his ancestors is made pointless by their own arguments. Yet Aurva persists in his intention, arguing that the suppression of righteous anger makes one incapable of upholding the social order (A 39) by punishing the bad and protecting the good (A 40).[33] Should he not exercise these functions, the world would be in danger from sin (A 50). But surely all these arguments are meaningless. Far from protecting the world or the good, Aurva is intent on destroying everyone.[34] Finally the problem of Aurva's revenge is resolved by the sophistry of his ancestors and the device of the horse-head fire.[35]

This motif, too, is but poorly integrated into its context. In many respects the Aurva story is quite similar, in its various motifs and in its general morphology, to the mythic cycle in which it is emboxed. The story is adduced by the sage Vasiṣṭha in order to discourage his grandson Parāśara from carrying out a plan of universal destruction very similar to that attributed to Aurva.[36] Parāśara, however, is motivated by the sudden and disillusioning revelation that the man he has thought to be his father is in fact his grandfather, and that his real father has been eaten by a demon.[37] As an initial reaction to this sudden shock, the plan does not strain credibility as does Aurva's belated and inconsistent vow. Moreover, Parāśara is quickly dissuaded from his plan by hearing the Aurvopākhyāna. He then turns his anger upon the rākṣasas, whom he holds responsible for his father's death. Parāśara then accordingly performs a genocidal sacrifice.[38] Finally, after destroying many of the demons, he is persuaded to desist, and he casts the sacrificial fire into the northern woods where it continues to burn, consuming the stones, trees, and demons.[39] His sacrifice is finally stopped through the intervention of several sages, including Pulastya the progenitor of the rākṣasas, who plead for their race and argue, like the departed Bhṛgus, that since Parāśara's own ancestors are rejoicing in heaven, they are in no need of an avenger (A 31).[40] All this makes good narrative sense. It is the attempt to use the Bhṛgus as both victims and intercessors that gives rise to the bizarre and unconvincing account of their racial suicide. Once again, the motif from the tale of Parāśara has been crudely adapted to the Aurva legend. Parāśara's shifting of his wrath from the general to the specific is thus devoid of the logical complications involved in Aurva's shift from specific to general.

There can hardly be any doubt that the Aurva episode, for all that it is cited as a precedent, is heavily under the influence of the Parāśara story and the whole cycle of Vāsiṣṭha myth. Its basic Bhārgava content, a story of violence and revenge, has been altered and overlaid with extraneous materials to suit the needs of a different mythic context. Nonetheless it is clear that the Aurva legend of the *Mahābhārata*, apart from its clumsy manipulation by the redactors of the Vāsiṣṭha cycle, was chosen by them because it exemplified the Bhārgava motif of annihilation.

For if Aurva is unable to pay back the murderous sons of Kṛtavīrya, vengeance is not to be denied his race. It is left to his descendant, the terrible Rāma Jāmadagnya, to pursue this mythic vendetta to its bloody conclusion.

Rāma, the only Bhārgava who actually kills anyone in the epic, is among the most violent characters in Sanskrit literature. He is an enigmatic figure, and despite the horrible deeds with which he is credited, he is the darling of the epic poets, who never tire of repeating his exploits.[41] The violence that he unleashes is unprecedented and exaggerated. According to the Āraṇyakaparvan version of his career, he kills his own mother, an act that seems to have no parallel in all the vast bulk of Sanskrit literature.[42] The major weight of Rāma's murderous temperament is, however, borne by the kṣatriyas.[43] His definitive action is the slaughter of the warrior class, which he accomplishes no fewer than twenty-one times.[44]

The parallels between the Rāma and Aurva episodes are many and have been observed many times.[45] Yet scholarly interpretations of the relationship between the two episodes have tended to ignore several of the motifs which they share and which, if properly observed, may further clarify that relationship.

Rāma's vengeance, like the unconsummated revenge of Aurva, has two distinct stages. In the first he pursues and kills Kārtavīrya for his violation of Jamadagni's ashram (R 47–48). In the second stage he repays the murder of his father with a genocidal crusade against the kṣatriyas (R 59–62). As in the Aurvopākhyāna (but not the story of Parāśara), Rāma's vengeance moves from the specific warriors who have injured him to the entire warrior class, most of whom have offended him in no way. Yet the story is so constructed, with the device of the two distinct provocations, that this progression, if incredible, is not illogical.

In both myths the outburst of generalized rage is stopped by the intervention of the spirits of departed Bhārgava sages (A 28–36,53–56; R 63). Now if, as appears to be the case, this motif in the Aurva episode has been adapted from a similar motif in the story of Parāśara, then, in the light of the obvious relation between the Rāma and Aurva episodes, it is likely that the former has borrowed it from the latter.[46]

Lords of Life

Closely associated with the theme of violent death is the motif of the return from death. Indeed, the motif of the magical restoration of life, together with its variants,[47] is as pervasive as any of the major motifs of the cycle. As with many of the motifs that figure significantly in Bhārgava mythology, the motif of the revival of the dead is by no means restricted to the corpus.[48] Yet, like the themes of death and violence, this theme, occurring sporadically throughout the mythological literature, has been included systematically in at least four Bhṛguid myths. A closely related motif, or perhaps a variant, the motif of a second birth from the body of someone other than one's mother, figures significantly in two Bhārgava episodes.

All the Bhṛgus and their wives (and fiancées) who die unnatural deaths, with the exception of those murdered by the kṣatriyas, are immediately restored to life. The power to accomplish this miracle is exercised by four different Bhṛgu sages,[49] who use it variously and not always on behalf of Bhṛgus. The ways in which this power is manifested vary from myth to myth and, in some cases, present features of interest.

The two beheaded Bhārgava wives, Reṇukā and Bhṛgu's wife, both regain their heads and their lives at the hands of their respective husbands. Reṇukā is restored by Jamadagni upon the request of Rāma (R 41–42) but the text does not explain how this miracle was performed. Jamadagni's ability to restore the dead is evidently to be accepted without comment as one of the many extraordinary powers developed by prolonged austerity.[50] The Rāma story, however, is alone among the numerous Bhārgava episodes in which this power is manifested in its disregard for technique. In the other stories, the techniques, which vary, are felt to be of great significance.

Bhṛgu's power to rejoin his wife's severed head and restore her to life is derived from a *satyakriyā*, an act of truth based upon the sage's perfect knowledge and conduct of dharma (ŚA 49). As such, it is a power derived from Bhṛgu's personal conduct, and presumably is exhausted temporarily by its exercise. Moreover, the power is not restricted to the resurrection of the dead; it could be applied to any miraculous feat.

Curiously, in another Bhārgava myth, this one from the *Mahābhārata*, it is stated unequivocally by a messenger of the gods that such an application of a satyakriyā is not possible. The story in which this occurs is the tale of the Bhārgava sage Ruru and his bride Pramadvarā.[51] Before her impending marriage the girl is bitten and killed by a snake,[52] and the grief-stricken sage attempts to perform a satyakriyā on the basis of his perfect brahmanical conduct:

> If I have performed severe penances, if I have fully gratified my elders, then by virtue of that let my dear one live. As I have been restrained and unwavering in my vows since birth, so may the charming Pramadvarā now rise up.[53]

But unlike the wife of Bhṛgu, Pramadvarā does not return to life. Instead, a messenger of the gods appears and tells Ruru, "These woeful words of yours are vain. Pious sage, one whose life is gone cannot live."[54] But the messenger says that there is yet a way, "devised long ago by the gods," whereby he may regain his lost love.[55] The plan is that Ruru may renounce half of his alotted span of life, which may then be lived out by his bride.[56] The plan is approved by Yama, and like Bhṛgu's wife, Pramadvarā rises as though from sleep.[57]

Although the method used by Bhṛgu in the *Matsyapurāṇa* and elsewhere is explicitly ruled out as impossible in the Ruru story, the method finally employed, like Bhṛgu's, is an extraordinary device used in an individual case.

In the major remaining Bhārgava myth involving resurrection, the myth of Śukra, Kaca, and Devayānī, the situation is somewhat different. There, it is said that the great Bhārgava sage possessed a secret spell whereby he could bring anyone back to life (ŚK 7–9 ff.). In fact, this spell is the central subject of the myth. The plot revolves around Kaca's attempt to learn the secret spell through his simultaneous discipleship under Śukra and courtship of Śukra's daughter. In the course of the charming story that develops, Śukra is shown using the spell repeatedly, on behalf both of his patrons the asuras and of Kaca. At the climax of the narrative, the spell changes hands and is used by Kaca to revive Śukra.

It is of particular interest that, despite the widespread occurrence of the theme of resurrection in the epic Bhārgava cycle, this spell, the *mṛtasaṃjīvinī vidyā*,[58] is associated only with Śukra and is not employed by the other Bhṛgus.[59] This association is confirmed by various epic and purāṇic sources;[60] yet in the myth in which Śukra's own mother is killed, no mention of this spell is to be found. Instead, Bhṛgu must intervene with a satyakriyā.

The reasons for this are complex, and show clearly how aware the Bhārgava mythmakers were that discreet motifs could be isolated. In the myth of Śukra and the asuras (ŚA), it is clearly stated that the important battle between the gods and the asuras can proceed only in the absence of Śukra, the asuras' guru and priest (ŚA 10). Further, in order to break the stalemate between the two parties, Śukra decides that he must depart to procure special mantras conducive to the victory of his patrons (ŚA 15). These mantras are said specifically to be unknown to Bṛhaspati, the gods' priest (ŚA 21), and to be obtainable only from Śiva (ŚA 15). These three qualifications can only refer to the mṛtasaṃjīvinī vidyā, which is known to have had them all.[61] Thus, Bhṛgu's wife is slain by Viṣṇu while her son is engaged in severe penance to procure the life-giving spell. Śukra is not then in a position to revive his mother and the miracle must be performed by Bhṛgu himself through other means.

But to raise explicitly the issue of the mṛtasaṃjīvinī vidyā after Bhṛgu's satyakriyā would create difficulties. It would serve to lessen the impact of Bhṛgu's miraculous performance and also would tend to draw attention away from the actual point of the episode, the betrayal of Śukra and the defeat of the asuras. Thus, though the motif serves its purpose when referred to in general terms, it would only get in the way if it were specified. The redactors of the myth chose, therefore, to suppress the identity of Śukra's wonderful spell, sacrificing specificity in order to mold the passage to their particular purpose.

The motif of resurrection is also conspicuous by its absence at some critical junctures of Bhārgava myth, especially in the two most violent stories, those of Aurva and Rāma. Aurva has no thought of reviving his slain ancestors, nor does Rāma attempt to restore life to his murdered father, despite the fact that he had previously instigated and witnessed Jamadagni's restoration of Reṇukā. The reason for this omission is clear: the motif is simply not wanted in these episodes. The point of both stories is the power of Bhārgava wrath. To revive the slain would be to deprive this wrath of its motivation.[62] In this light it is significant that, through the otherwise pointless episode of Renukā's death and resurrection, the Bhārgava mythmakers have included this important motif in the story of Rāma Jāmadagnya.

The Second Birth

Śukra, the master of the mṛtasaṃjīvinī vidyā, figures in two myths, his encounters with Kaca (ŚK) and with Śiva (ŚŚ), that contain a curious motif, that of second birth. This is doubtless related to the motif of resurrection. In these stories a figure is swallowed and then disgorged. The disgorgement is regarded as a special kind of birth, and the two figures, the swallower and the swallowed, are established in a new filial relationship.[63]

As in many areas of Bhārgava myth, the motif is flexible enough for Śukra to assume the roles of both swallower and swallowed. Of the two episodes, the encounter of Śukra and Kaca is by far the more elaborate and, indeed, the more lucid. In the course of his discipleship with the great Bhārgava, Kaca, the son of his teacher's archrival, undergoes many ordeals. Finally, Śukra unwittingly swallows him (ŚK 33). This leads ultimately to the transfer of the precious saṃjīvinī vidyā from master to pupil. By having come forth from his guru's body, Kaca becomes the son of Śukra (ŚK 48). The point is stressed and made more explicit in the chapter following the one in which Kaca gains the mantra. Devayānī, Śukra's daughter, begs Kaca to marry her. He refuses finally on the grounds of his new relationship with Śukra, which, he claims, makes her his sister. "Where you once dwelt, O charming, long-eyed, moon-faced, lovely girl, there, in Kāvya's belly, have I too dwelt. You who are my sister according to dharma ought not speak in this way."[64]

By contrast with this elaborate episode, Śukra's encounter with Śiva is terse and obscure. It is clear, however, that Śukra, having been swallowed and expelled by Śiva, is regarded as having thereby become the son of the god and of his consort (ŚŚ 34–35). The two episodes differ in many respects. However, one important point in the context of Bhārgava myth is that the issue of death and resurrection is central to the myth of Śukra and Kaca and yet absent from the myth of Śukra and Śiva. While the purpose and result of Kaca's second birth are made clear, those of Śukra's are only partially so.

At the end of the Śukra and Śiva narrative it is said that Śukra attained the state that he desired (ŚŚ 37), but the sage's desire is only inferable from the myth itself. What he actually attains in the encounter is the status of the son of Śiva and Umā and a concomitant state of invulnerability (ŚŚ 35). He is also said to have increased in wealth (ŚŚ 26).[65] The myth itself is narrated in response to a question as to how Sukra attained greatness (ŚŚ 4), and it provides only a partial answer, in that the episode presupposes enormous power on his part.

It is worthy of note that the power, wealth, and invulnerability that Śukra manages to attain as a result of this mysterious and hostile encounter with Śiva are the same boons the god grants him in recompense for his severe penances in the myth of Śukra and the asuras (ŚA 62–65). Both myths avoid mention of the saṃjīvinī vidyā; yet the relation of the boons in the two episodes, and the identity established between the mantras of the asuras' myth and the secret vidyā of the Kaca myth, coupled with the recurrence of the motif of the second birth in the Kaca and Śiva myths, would seem to establish that the three episodes are intimately connected. The key to that connection must be the relation of Śukra to Śiva and the sage's unique mastery of the secret life-giving magic.

Observations

The mythology of the Bhārgavas is to an extraordinary degree concerned with the themes of death and resurrection. The distribution of these themes in the cycle suggests that the myths may be separated into two major groups concerned chiefly with violent death and with resurrection, respectively. In myths of the former group, epitomized by the stories of Aurva and Rāma, conflict is established between the Bhṛgus and the kṣatriyas. Violence is genocidal, and the motif of the revival of the dead is absent or of peripheral significance. Myths of the latter group are chiefly concerned with the figure of Uśanas Kāvya, the great Śukra. In these myths conflict is established between the Bhṛgus and the gods. Violence is less pronounced and involves individuals. Those who die are invariably restored to life by one means or another.

There is no absolute distinction between the groups, since themes and even specific motifs may be found diffused throughout the cycle. Moreover, several important myths do not conform well to either type. Nonetheless, it appears that these groups do represent two important nuclei of Bhārgava myth and their isolation and analysis may serve to shed new light on the origins and development of the Bhārgava cycle.

2

Masters of the Earth: The Bhṛgus and the Kṣatriyas

The myths of the Bhārgavas may be catalogued in a number of ways, depending upon the themes of greatest interest to the cataloguer. Thus, for example, the cycle may be roughly divided into two portions, according to the distribution and use of the themes of death and resurrection. A similar significant division in the corpus can be observed with regard to the ways in which the myths express a sense of relation between the Bhṛgus and other groups.

The issue of a relational stance was obviously of the greatest importance to the Bhārgava mythmakers. Virtually every major Bhārgava episode from the literature, purāṇic, as well as epic, attempts to cope with the ambivalences of such a stance in what appears to be an effort to define the group's place in the social and spiritual orders of brahmanical India.

Accordingly, the cycle may again be regarded as having two separate but closely interrelated phases, one concerning the relations of the Bhṛgus and the kṣatriyas, the other the relations of the Bhṛgus and the gods. Like the other aspects of the Bhārgava cycle, these two are not wholly mutually exclusive. Several important Bhṛgus are shown in different myths as engaged in struggles over status and dominance with both the princes and the gods. In a few cases the same myth involves relational issues with regard to both groups. Few Bhārgava myths are wholly free of these issues.

As with the themes of life and death, these relational questions are not unique to the Bhārgava cycle.[1] What is unique is the degree to which these questions become the central concern of the myths of the Bhṛgus. Indeed, questions of status, dominance, and function assume the character of an obsession with the Bhārgavas.

Also peculiar is the strong ambivalence that characterizes the relations between Bhṛgus and non-Bhṛgus. The relations of the Bhṛgus with both the kṣatriyas and the gods range from the most intimate friendship to the most murderous hostility. Between these extremes are a number of highly significant attempts at reconciliation.

The tensions that are developed between the Bhṛgus and non-Bhārgava groups and the attempts to alleviate them shed considerable light on problems of the identity of the Bhṛgus and their role in the formation of the *Mahābhārata*.

Of the two groups, kṣatriyas and gods, it is the former whose relations with the Bhṛgus present the most complexity and ambivalence.

Priests and Warriors: Bhārgava-Kṣatriya Conflict

Of all the repeated themes that characterize Bhārgava myths, the one that has captured the interest and the imagination of scholars almost exclusively is the violent conflict between the clan and the warrior class, especially as this theme is represented in the career of the Bhārgava Rāma.[2] It is this theme, too, that has chiefly gripped the fancy of the Bhārgava mythmakers.[3] The theme in its most fully developed form is expressed in the subcycle of myths centering about the Bhṛguid branch represented by the sages Aurva, Ṛcīka, Jamadagni, and Rāma. The myths of this subcycle concern a complex series of relations between these sages and two kṣatriya families, the Haihayas and the Kauśikas. This is the only area of Bhṛguid myth in which great stress is laid on genealogy.[4] As a result, the conflict between the Bhṛgus and the Haihayas takes on something of the nature of a family feud, handed down from generation to generation. The degree to which the conflict pervades the Bhārgava corpus and the severity of the conflict mark it as an issue of particular concern to the Bhṛgus.

The theme is most fully elaborated in the Aurvopākhyāna and the various versions of the career of the Bhārgava Rāma. In both myths tension between the Bhārgavas and the descendants of the king Kṛtavīrya results in an attempt at genocide. This theme, however, is inverted, and the perpetrators and victims are reversed. The inversion, when viewed in the context of Bhārgava genealogy, has given rise to the tradition that Rāma's slaughter of the kṣatriyas constitutes the Bhṛgus' revenge for the massacre of Aurva's time, a revenge that is thus delayed for three generations.[5]

There are, however, several points that render this tradition suspect. For example, none of the elaborate epic versions of the Rāma myth makes any mention of Aurva or the extermination of the Bhṛgus.[6] The motive for Rāma's campaign in all these versions is revenge for the murder of Jamadagni.

The Aurva and Rāma myths largely define the theme of the Bhārgava's conflict with the kṣatriyas. They do not, however, exhaust it. One other major Bhṛgu, the sage Cyavana, is seen to be in conflict with at least two kings. In an epic account of his encounter with the Aśvins, he visits great hardships upon the people of the king Śaryāti in retaliation for his injury at the hands of the king's daughter (C 14–16).[7] In order to calm Cyavana's anger the king must humbly propitiate him and give him his daughter in marriage (C 23–26). The sage is also involved in a lengthy campaign of provocation against the king Kuśika, during which the sage inflicts insult, indignity, and even physical abuse upon the king and his queen. The royal pair, however, manage to avoid the Bhārgava's wrath by steadfastly enduring these provocations without complaint.[8] The provocations are intended to enable Cyavana to carry out his plan for the destruction of the Kauśika line.[9]

Priests and Patrons

The relations of the Bhṛgus and the kṣatriyas are not wholly hostile, but are characterized by a marked ambivalence. In virtually every case of conflict between the groups, episodes of hostility are in immediate proximity to others indicative of friendly and even intimate relations.

The normative relationship among the four varṇas of Indian society, as prescribed and lauded in the Sanskrit texts, is one in which each group discharges its class function. Princes are to rule, protect the people, uphold the good, and above all, honor and support the brahmans. The brahmans are expected to study the Vedas and other sacred texts and perform sacrifices on behalf of their royal patrons. Thus, in cooperation with the other classes, the brahmans and kṣatriyas establish and uphold the social, political, and spiritual order. This is the relationship that is said to have existed between the Bhṛgus and the princes of the very families with whom their conflict is so severe.

The massacre of the Bhṛgus arises from the fact that they were the sacrificial priests of Kṛtavīrya, and were richly rewarded for their services (A 1–2). These amicable relations change when Kṛtavīrya's sons covet the wealth that he has so liberally bestowed on the Bhṛgus. In the myth of Cyavana (C), the sage's relations with the king Śaryāti proceed from hostile to cordial. After the king has propitiated the angry sage and given him his daughter, the sage, by way of conciliation, offers to perform a sacrifice for him (C 56).

These two episodes can be connected on the basis of the genealogies of both the Bhṛgus and the kṣatriyas. Although neither the Aurva nor the Cyavana story mentions it, other epic passages state that Aurva is the son of Cyavana,[10] while Kṛtavīrya and the Haihayas are descended from Śaryāti.[11] Elsewhere in the *Mahābhārata* the king Vītahavya, another descendant of Śaryāti, is said to have been granted protection from his enemies by Bhṛgu himself, and, interestingly enough, to have actually become a Bhṛgu through the power of the sage.[12] It would appear from these references that the epic preserves a tradition, known to the Vedas, of the Bhṛgus as the traditional purohitas of the Haihayas and Tālajaṅghas, the descendants through Śaryāti of the legendary first king, Manu.[13]

On the other hand, reference to this tradition is wholly lacking in the elaborate accounts of the conflict involving the Haihaya monarch Arjuna Kārtavīrya and the Bhārgava sages Jamadagni and Rāma. In these the king is received with due hospitality at Jamadagni's ashram, but no special relation between the two groups is noted. Unlike other Bhārgava myths concerned with kṣatriyas, the Rāma story is free from ambivalence.[14]

The sages descended from Cyavana are further remarkable for the fact that, despite the tension between them and the warrior class, they almost unanimously take kṣatriya wives. In some cases these marriages originate in the tension between the groups. Cyavana, the founder of a Bhārgava subbranch, is best known as the husband of Sukanyā, the daughter of Śaryāti (C 24–27).[15] The king gives his daughter away to the decrepit sage without hesitation, but only because of his fear of him (C 14–26).

Elsewhere in the *Mahābhārata* Cyavana is said to have married a woman named Āruṣī, who is described as the "daughter of Manu."[16] It is not clear whether this is in fact a second wife or merely another reference to Sukanyā.[17] The question is of interest because Āruṣī is said to be the mother of Aurva.[18] If Āruṣī and Sukanyā are one and the same, then Cyavana's branch of the Bhṛgus are cousins of their patrons (and archenemies) the Haihayas.

Aurva is said to have been the father of Ṛcīka (CK 29), but his wife is not identified in the epic. Ṛcīka, too, marries a kṣatriya princess in an episode made particularly interesting because of the peculiar bride price demanded by her father (R 4–12).[19] The bride is the Kauśika princess Satyavatī, the daughter of Gādhi (R 3–4).[20] This union, too, is of special significance for Bhārgava mythology in that it joins the Bhṛgus with the race of the important figure Viśvāmitra. Ṛcīka's son, Jamadagni, follows the family tradition by asking for the hand of Reṇukā, the daughter of a king named Prasenajit (R 26).[21] Their son Rāma remains celibate in the epic.

These marriages of Cyavana and his descendants are of interest in the context of the traditions of the Dharmaśāstra. According to the *Manusmṛti*, for example, the offspring of unions in which the wife is of a lower varṇa than her husband are said to be *apasadas*, or somewhat degraded members of their fathers' varṇas.[22] According to this dictum Aurva, Jamadagni, and Rāma at the least are to be considered *brāhmaṇāpasadas*, degraded brahmans, while it is likely that the same is true for the rest of the subbranch if not the entire Bhārgava race.[23]

The tendency to marry nonbrahmans is not restricted to the line of Cyavana. In fact it is difficult to find a single case in the literature of any Bhṛgu marrying a brahman. Bhṛgu himself is associated, in the epics and Purāṇas, with various wives, all of whom appear to be of supernatural origin. In the *Mahābhārata* he is said to have married Pulomā, on whom he fathers Cyavana.[24] Her parentage is not clear, but there is some evidence that she is the daughter of a demon.[25] Śukra is said to have married Jayantī, the daughter of Indra (ŚA 76).[26]

Several of the lesser Bhṛgus also take wives of nonbrahman origin. In the story of Ruru it is related that the sage married Pramadvarā, daughter of the celestial nymph (*apsaras*) Menakā by Viśvāvasu, king of the heavenly musicians (*gandharvas*),[27] while his mother is said to have been the nymph Ghṛtācī.[28]

This peculiarity of Bhṛgu marriages is corroborated and heightened by the fact that Śukra's daughter Devayānī, one of the few Bhārgava women with a major role in the mythic cycle, is married to the king Yayāti. As Sukthankar observed, this is "one of the few *pratiloma* marriages on record in Brahmanical literature."[29]

The Warrior-Priest

The sages of Cyavana's line not only serve the ruling class as its priests and marry its women; they take upon themselves one of the central functions of the kṣatriyas, the mastery of the arts of war. By their actions, certain Bhṛgus, especially Rāma, virtually become kṣatriyas. In this respect they are set apart from every other brahman family of Indian myth.[30]

Just as the knowledge of the mṛtasaṃjīvinī vidyā is the special province of Śukra, so is *dhanurveda*, the science of weaponry, human and divine, the peculiar preserve of the descendants of Cyavana. The dhanurveda is said to have been mastered and transmitted in turn by Aurva, Rçīka, Jamadagni, and Rāma.

Aurva's possession of the science of arms is not well established in the epic. There is no mention of it whatever in the Aurvopākhyāna, where the sage's anger is expressed in typically brahmanical fashion. Elsewhere in the *Mahābhārata*, in the debate between the wind-god and Arjuna Kārtavīrya, archenemy of the Bhṛgus, it is said that Aurva exterminated the Tālajaṅgha line of kṣatriyas all by himself. However, the way in which this feat is accomplished is not specified. Aurva's mastery of the dhanurveda is well known in the Purāṇas[31] but in those texts is perhaps merely an innovation based upon the association of other Bhṛgus with martial skills.

In the epic tradition, Bhārgava mastery of the dhanurveda begins with Ṛcīka. In the Anuśāsanaparvan's account of Aurva's descendants, Cyavana himself states that the entire dhanurveda revealed itself to Ṛcīka and that for the destruction of the kṣatriyas he mastered it and passed it on to his son Jamadagni (CK 29–31). The Āraṇyakaparvan version of the origins and career of Rāma states that the dhanurveda, including knowledge of the various missiles, was revealed to Jamadagni (R 24). This is in keeping with the description of the sage given in the Anuśāsanaparvan as practicing his archery and threatening, convincingly, to shoot down the sun.[32] These passages seem hardly in keeping with the fact that the sage is murdered "like a deer in the forest" by the sons of Kārtavīrya in the Āraṇyakaparvan version itself. (R 50). On the other hand, the Śāntiparvan version of Rāma's career is at pains to indicate that Jamadagni was an extremely tranquil sage immersed in his austerities,[33] while his son Rāma was the great master of the dhanurveda.[34]

There are a number of reasons for the discrepancies among these accounts. To a certain extent the different provenance of the two major accounts of Rāma's career may be the cause of the differing characterizations of Jamadagni.[35] Still other versions have tampered with the details of the story for various reasons. Thus, for example, the Anuśāsanaparvan's attribution of the acquisition of the dhanurveda to Rçīka contributes to the notion of an ongoing Bhārgava-kṣatriya feud from Aurva's time to Rāma's.

Notwithstanding the various accounts of who first received the dhanurveda, all versions are in agreement as to the purpose of the revelation. The culmination of the Bhṛgus' knowledge of military skills is Rāma's extermination of the kṣatriyas. Although several of his forebears are said to have mastered the dhanurveda, they do so only that they may pass it on; it is Rāma alone who puts this knowledge to use. He is the only Bhṛgu, indeed the only mythic sage except Droṇa, who actually uses the weapons of the kṣatriyas to destroy them. Thus although Ṛcīka and Jamadagni are unusual, Rāma is truly unique, a brahman who behaves like a kṣatriya and who defeats the kṣatriyas on their own ground.

An understanding of this aberrant and enigmatic figure must surely, then, illuminate the Bhārgava-kṣatriya themes of the cycle. Rāma and his career of genocide are unquestionably the culmination of that aspect of the corpus. Indeed, this figure has established himself as the single most significant Bhārgava in the *Mahābhārata* and in Indian mythological literature in general.

At the end of his very unbrahmanical career Rāma, by virtue of his extirpation of the ruling class, becomes the de facto lord of the earth (R 64).[36] Yet he does not exercise kingly rule. For him to do so would strike at the roots of the normative social system of the epics and law texts in a way that even the martial pursuits of the Bhārgavas do not. Thus in all versions Rāma presents the newly conquered earth to the brahmans led by Kaśyapa, who, in one way or another, manage to reestablish princely rule.[37]

The Bhārgava redactors of the *Mahābhārata* repeatedly show their desire to provide an explanation for the appearance of a martial hero in a line of contemplative sages. This desire and the forms that their explanations take are among the most provocative and instructive features of the epic literature. In order to explain Rāma's deviance from the varṇāśramadharma the redactors had recourse to the other most widely known example of such deviance in the mythological literature, the career of Viśvāmitra. By integrating the two episodes, they have achieved an interesting sort of mythological economy whereby the two examples of deviance are traced to a single cause, and the two figures to a common ancestor. In this way two important and originally separate mythic cycles and families, the Bhārgava and the Kauśika, have been made to intersect at a critical point. The warlike disposition of the brahman Rāma and the brahmanical inclinations of the prince Viśvāmitra are seen as mirror images produced by a unique inversion.

The inversion occurs in the operation of a double boon given by Bhṛgu or Ṛcīka to the wife and to the daughter of the Kauśika monarch Gādhi. Gādhi's daughter, Satyavatī, is married to Ṛcīka, and the sage (in some versions Bhṛgu) offers a boon whereby she is to bear a son who will exemplify the brahmanical qualities. Her mother, through the same boon, is to give birth to a perfect exemplar of the knightly virtues. The device that confers the boon is confused, intentionally in some versions, so that the sons bearing the promised virtues are given to the "wrong" mothers. Satyavatī is horrified at the thought that she will bear a bloodthirsty brahman and prevails upon the granter of the boon to postpone its effects, in her case, for one generation. As a result

Viśvāmitra, her brother, is a kṣatriya interested only in the brahmanical life, while her grandson Rāma is a brahman who delights in war.

This confusing episode is evidently of the greatest significance for the epic redactors, as it is repeated with different details no fewer than four times in the *Mahābhārata*.[38] The contexts of the different versions are of some interest. Two versions are related in response to questions touching only upon the career of the Bhārgava Rāma.[39] In these no interest is shown in that of his counterpart, and in one of them Viśvāmitra is not even mentioned by name. A third, highly condensed version is narrated ostensibly in response to a question concerning the peculiarities of both heroes, but is unquestionably purely Bhārgava in purpose.[40] Only one of the versions introduces the career of Viśvāmitra.[41] Since three of the four accounts show no real interest in Viśvāmitra but simply use the story to explain the peculiarity of Rāma, it would appear that the motif of the switched boons is of greater significance to the Bhārgava cycle than to the Kauśika. This is further suggested by the fact that while this complex Bhārgava-Kauśika episode is the only explanation offered in the literature for Rāma's unbrahmanical character, there are a number of other elaborate stories that explain Viśvāmitra's metamorphosis without any reference to Rāma or the Bhārgavas.[42]

Moreover, despite the efforts of the Bhārgava mythmakers to depict the careers of Rāma and Viśvāmitra as parallel but inverted phenomena, there are some important discrepancies between them that betray the hand of the mythmaker. First, the switch of varṇa-role is not exactly parallel in the two cases. All the epic sources agree that Viśvāmitra, the Kauśika prince, actually became a brahman.[43] On the other hand, none of the many versions of the Rāma story nor any of the references to Rāma that are scattered thickly throughout the *Mahābhārata* suggest that the Bhārgava hero actually renounced his class to become a kṣatriya. At most, it is stated that he is a *kṣatravṛttir brāhmaṇaḥ*, a brahman who acts like a kṣatriya (R 19). The difference is significant, as it shows that the two terms of the boon actually operate in different ways.

A second curious discrepancy is the asymmetric postponement of the boon's effects for one generation only in the case of the Bhārgavas.[44]

On the basis of these discrepancies, as well as the fact that the Satyavatī episode is of unquestionably Bhārgava origin, it appears more than likely that the whole episode was devised at some point after the establishment of the Rāma and Viśvāmitra myths as a rationale for both, but especially the former. The creation and diffusion of the Satyavatī episode, and its linking of the Rāma and Viśvāmitra myths[45] on the basis of the inversion motif, is a characteristic example of metamythology. By means of such creations the Bhārgava mythmakers and epic redactors were able to elaborate the Bhṛguid myths and integrate them, for their own ends, into the pseudohistorical framework of the *Mahābhārata*.

Perhaps the most illuminating example of such metamyth in the great epic is to be found in one of the other versions of the Satyavatī story. This version forms the prophetic culmination of the Cyavanakuśikasaṃvāda (CK), the dialogue between Cyavana and the king Kuśika, which occupies chapters 52–56 of the Anuśāsanaparvan. The passage is nothing less than an attempt to synthesize all the diverse ambivalent contacts between the Bhṛgus and the kṣatriyas into a coherent whole, in an effort to resolve the discrepancies and contradictions among the various elements of the Bhārgava cycle. The effort is a noble one, but because it is not wholly successful and because it has not replaced the other, contradictory versions, it betrays the hand and the mind of the Bhārgava redactors as do few other passages in the literature.

The basic narrative of the passage involves a curious confrontation between the sage Cyavana, the founder of the race of Rāma, and the king Kuśika, the eponymous ancestor of Viśvāmitra's line. As such, it is yet another example of the clash between Bhārgava and kṣatriya that demonstrates the superiority of the former. Yet this is by far the least interesting aspect of the episode.

The story is related by Bhīṣma in response to the never-failing curiosity of Yudhiṣṭhira on the subject of Rāma's career. This time, however, the prince evinces interest in the career of Viśvāmitra as well. This is the only point in the epic at which a frame-story question specifically involves both figures (CK 1–6).[46] Bhīṣma does not, in fact, directly answer Yudhiṣṭhira's questions. Instead he begins the curious tale of Cyavana and Kuśika.

The Bhārgava sage, perceiving that some injury would befall his race, decided to destroy the race of the Kauśikas (CK 8–9). Thereupon he approached the king Kuśika and announced his intention of living with him.[47] There ensues a long and fairly complex narrative of how the Bhārgava attempted to provoke the king and his queen by means of various insults, indignities, and injuries. Kuśika, however, is not to be provoked, and by his humble endurance of the sage's insults he finally succeeds in propitiating him. Cyavana offers the king a boon, and the latter requests an explanation of the Bhārgava's strange behavior.[48]

Cyavana's explanation is equally strange. He states that he had heard from the god Brahman that, because of the hostility between the brahmans and the kṣatriyas, a mixing of the two races would come about, and also that Kuśika's grandson would be born endowed with brilliance and valor. Therefore, he says, he had come in order to protect his own race by destroying the Kauśikas (CK, 10–13).[49]

This explanation is extremely interesting in the context of the other Bhārgava myths that fill the epic. Nowhere else in the extensive Bhārgava corpus are the Bhṛgus said to be threatened by the Kauśikas. Kṣatriya violence against them is exclusively the preserve of the Haihayas, the descendants of Kārtavīrya. Yet the latter group find no mention in this episode. Although it is true that as a result of miscegenation the mighty Viśvāmitra is said in the Bhārgava accounts to have arisen in the Kauśika line, nowhere is it said that that enigmatic figure poses any threat to the Bhṛgus. Indeed, if he is infamous among brahmans it is because of his enmity for his old rival Vasiṣṭha and his race. Moreover, it is odd that a horror of *varṇasaṃkara*, a mixing of the classes, should be expressed by Cyavana who, in his own proper myth, is said to have been himself the husband of at least one kṣatriya princess. In the face of this obscure provocation, then, Cyavana had decided upon the typically Bhṛguid solution of genocide.

The sage desists from his plan, however, and perceiving that Kuśika's deepest desire is for the brahmanical life (CK, 14–15), he announces that his grandson will indeed be a brahman (CK, 17–18). Kuśika asks how this is to come about, and Cyavana offers an explanation of paramount interest, as it is nothing less than a conspectus of the Bhārgava mythology of his own line from Aurva to Rāma. It is the only such passage in the epic and it is as striking for its content as for the fact that an entire subcycle of Bhārgava myth is here restructured by a Bhṛguid sage.

Cyavana begins with a short version of the Aurva myth agreeing essentially with the outlines it has in the Aurvopākhyāna.[50] He then goes on to prophesy the future of his line, saying that the dhanurveda will be revealed to Ṛcīka and handed down to Jamadagni for the destruction of the warrior class. He then refers briefly to the Satyavatī episode and the births of Rāma and Viśvāmitra, promising brahmanhood to Kuśika in the third generation (CK 29–36). Kuśika is delighted with this promise and Cyavana takes his leave. Bhīṣma concludes the passage by stating that he has related in full the cause of the connection between the Bhṛgus and the Kauśikas, and that the births of Rāma and Viśvāmitra came about as predicted (CK 37–42).

Cyavana's prophecy is unique among all the versions of Bhārgava myth in that it provides a coherent genealogy of his branch of the Bhṛgus in terms of its ambivalent relationship to the kṣatriyas. It is the only passage that explicitly connects the Aurva story with the Bhārgavas' acquisition and transmission of the dhanurveda and with the career of Rāma, while at the same time providing a rationale for Rāma's aberrant behavior. As such, it should be of great help in explaining structural interrelationships in this portion of the cycle. In fact, it is of value in this way largely because it fails in its stated purposes and shows clear evidence of thematic manipulation on the part of its authors.

The secondary nature of the episode is first noticeable in the fact that despite the length and complexity of the encounter between Cyavana and Kuśika,[51] the story does not really explain the Rāma-Viśvāmitra inversion at all. Cyavana's original purpose was to prevent the confusion of the varṇas that he foresaw. However, he abandons this purpose, and the only explanations he is able to offer are (1) that the hostility between the Bhṛgus and the kṣatriyas and the Bhṛgus' acquisition of the dhanurveda come about for "divinely fated reasons" (CK 25–30), and (2) that "two women" will cause the exchange of varṇa-roles (CK 35). Cyavana's function in the episode is purely informational. Since the information that he does provide is elliptical and presupposes knowledge of the other versions, it is evident that the passage is posterior to at least one of them.

Yet Cyavana does not merely summarize earlier versions of the myth; he attempts to rationalize the discrepancies of the more extensive versions. The most transparent of these attempts concerns the problem of the asymmetric skipping of a generation in the appearance of the results of Bhṛgu's boon. The motif of the skipped generation, whereby Rāma and not his father becomes the kṣatravṛttir brāhmaṇaḥ, is nowhere else applied to the Kauśika geneology. Yet in Yudhiṣṭhira's question, which begins the passage, the Pāṇḍava prince asks how the exchange of class roles, which he calls a *doṣa*, a flaw or irregularity, skipped the sons and appeared only in the grandsons (CK 6). The interpolation of the motif of the skipped generation on the Kauśika side is stressed by repetition; Cyavana twice promises Kuśika that his race will attain brahmanhood in the "third generation" (CK 18–19,36).

This new symmetry is accomplished simply by the substitution of Kuśika, the grandfather of Viśvāmitra, for his father Gādhi as the ancestor in whose generation the "cause" of the switch occurs. In aid of this substitution, the story of Gādhi and, indeed, the entire account of the switched boons is suppressed, surviving only in the cryptic reference to the "two women." Clearly the establishment of this symmetry, and the elimination of the old discrepancy, is one of the major purposes of the episode. Yet the substitution itself gives rise to further difficulties. For if the episode of Satyavatī and her mother is suppressed, then there can be no clear frame of genealogical reference whereby Rāma can be established as belonging to the "third generation." This lack seems to be made good by the passage's tradition of the dhanurveda, revealed to Ṛcīka, as being merely transmitted by

Jamadagni. Thus Rāma inherits his martial skill in the third generation.

The result of this manipulation is clear and may be summarized succinctly: the choice of Kuśika rather than Gādhi as the central kṣatriya figure, the one who first conceived a desire for brahmanhood, coupled with the suppression of the details of the origin of Rāma's martial character, provides an integral and symmetrical pattern whereby both Rāma and Viśvāmitra may be shown as having given up their family traditions in the "third generation."[52]

The authors of the Cyavanakuśikasaṃvāda, however, were not content with a simple readjustment of the Rāma-Viśvāmitra story. Their purpose was the emendation of the prior tradition of Bhārgava-kṣatriya relations and a new synthesis of that tradition with the secondary legend of the Bhārgava-Kauśika switch. To accomplish this purpose they have radically departed from tradition by substituting the Kauśikas for the Haihayas, the traditional patrons and enemies of the Bhṛgus. This connection of the Kauśikas to the Bhṛgus is obscure. This tendentious process is accomplished in two steps.

First, all specific reference to the old enemies of the Bhṛgus is eliminated. Throughout the passage the patrons of the Bhṛgus, the perpetrators of the Bhārgava massacre, and the principle objects of Bhārgava wrath, elsewhere identified as descendants of Kṛtavīrya, are identified only by the generic term, kṣatriya (CK 25–26,30). Further, the frame story, the confrontation of Cyavana and Kuśika, posits a hostility between the Bhārgavas and the Kauśikas that is resolved and turned into amity as a result of Kuśika's submission to the Bhṛgu sage. This amity is expressed in the intermarriage between the two races. The inevitable implication of the sequence is that the Kauśikas have taken the place of the Haihayas.

Yet in order to effect this synthesis, the mythmakers have had to do violence to the mythic traditions that they have sought to bring together. Not only has the episode of Satyavatī's boon been suppressed, but the very point of the Bhārgava-Haihaya mythos has been completely eliminated. For, although Cyavana is minutely interested in relating the reasons for the Bhṛgus' acquisition of the dhanurveda and the way in which they preserved and transmitted it "for the destruction of the kṣatriyas" (CK 30), he carefully omits any mention of Rāma's slaughter of the warrior class (CK 33).

The omission is startling in the light of the preoccupation that the Bhārgava mythmakers elsewhere evince for this myth, and because of the apparent thrust of Cyavana's prediction. It is clear that the authors of this passage have set out (CK 24–33) to lead up to Rāma's bloody feat as the culminating act in the vendetta they have envisioned. Yet here, where it would seem most appropriate, the formula *triḥsaptakṛtvaḥ pṛthivīṃ kṛtvā niḥkṣatriyāṃ purā*, "having long ago twenty-one times freed the earth of kṣatriyas," the favorite of the epic bards,[53] is conspicuous by its absence. Cyavana hastily ends his truncated narration and shows a sudden desire to leave quickly.

This abrupt termination of the account of the Bhṛgus is in fact necessitated by the Bhārgava-Kauśika synthesis developed in the episode. It shows that the authors were fully aware of the implications of their manipulations. For the ostensible point of the passage is the union of the Bhṛgus and the kṣatriya Kauśikas. Therefore it would hardly do for Cyavana to end his conciliatory explanation to Kuśika by telling him that his race, indeed his entire class, is to be annihilated by a Bhārgava. To do so would be to stress the contradictions with which the passage is filled. Instead, the sage returns to the subject of the birth of Viśvāmitra and the episode draws to an end.

The Cyavanakuśikasaṃvāda is an outstanding example of the phenomenon of metamyth, and its significance for the study of the growth and function of the corpus cannot be too highly stressed. Not only is it a "myth" whose subject is myth, a myth about myth, but it shows, more clearly than any other part of the Bhārgava cycle, the sensitivity to thematic material and the conscious manipulation of the corpus that have set the cycle apart from the other mythology of the *Mahābhārata*.

Viśvāmitra's change of status from kṣatriya to brahman, despite the fascination it exerted on the narrators of the Rāma story, is not the example of such a change most intimately associated with the Bhārgava cycle. Chapter 31 of the Anuśāsanaparvan relates the story of the king Vītahavya who, through the direct intervention of Bhṛgu, becomes a brahman and the founder of a Bhārgava line.[54] The Vītahavya story is particularly interesting in that it is thematically quite similar to the myths of the Aurva-Rāma cycle and presents yet another example of the motif and thematic inversion that characterize the cycle. It concerns the wars of Vītahavya and his kin, the descendants of the Śāryāta king Hehaya,[55] with the ruling house of Kāśī. After repeated defeats at the hand of the Haihayas,[56] Divodāsa, the king of Kāśī, takes refuge in the ashram of the sage Bharadvāja,[57] where an extraordinary son, Pratardana, is born to him.[58] Pratardana masters the entire dhanurveda and in one battle single-handedly slaughters all the sons of Vītahavya with his crescent arrows.[59] Vītahavya, his sons slain, abandons his capital and flees to the ashram of Bhṛgu. The sage offers him refuge.[60] Pratardana, pursuing the king, comes to the hermitage and tells Bhṛgu to deliver Vītahavya up on the grounds that he has exterminated the royal race of Kāśī.[61] Pratardana argues that only by killing Vītahavya will he be able to discharge his debt to his own father.[62]

Bhṛgu, moved by compassion for the fugitive, replies that there are no kṣatriyas in his ashram, only brahmans.[63] Since a sage of the stature of Bhṛgu cannot tell a lie or utter vain words, reality must conform to his speech. Vītahavya becomes a brahman from that moment.[64] Pratardana retires, pleased that he has forced his enemy out of the warrior class.[65] Vīthavya, a brahman by the mere word of Bhṛgu, becomes a brahmanical seer, an expounder of brahman, and the founder of a Bhārgava branch whose descendants include Pramati, Ruru, and Śaunaka.[66]

Clearly this story, in which the races of the Bhṛgus and the Haihayas are once more mingled, is but another link in the chain of episodes that connect them, and presents a partial inversion of the Aurva-Rāma cycle. In the other myths a branch of the Bhṛgus is seen to be descended from the kṣatriyas, and its foremost hero is a brahman who acts like a murderous warrior. In the Vītahavya episode it is a particularly murderous warrior who becomes a brahman and the founder of a Bhārgava line. The references to mutual genocide that occur in the Vītahavya story are also strongly reminiscent of those of the Aurva-Rāma cycle. Pratardana, the wonderful warrior boy and precocious master of the dhanurveda who seeks to gratify his father by the slaughter of the Haihayas, is virtually the model of the Bhārgava Rāma. Both heroes are said to fight alone and to dispatch their enemies with *bhallas*, a special kind of crescent-shaped arrow.[67] The similarities between the myths cannot be coincidental.

3
The Masters of Heaven: The Bhṛgus and the Gods

The Bhārgava myths dealing with the kṣatriyas, especially the subcycle of the descendants of Cyavana, serve basically to establish a stance. The relations of the Bhṛgus to the ruling class in all their ambivalence and baroque complexity finally point to an attitude of Bhārgava dominance. This concern, amounting to an obsession, with the kṣatriyas leaves little room for other areas of Bhārgava interest and it is a particularly notable feature of the central Aurva-Rāma cycle that the gods and other supernatural beings that swarm through most epic myth are here largely absent.[1]

On the other hand, the remainder of the Bhārgava cycle, especially the myths dealing with the deeds of Bhṛgu, Śukra, and Cyavana, are as obsessed with the gods and other supernatural beings as the Aurva-Rāma subcycle is with the kṣatriyas, exhibiting, for the most part, little interest in the warrior class. The two groups of myths, then, are complementary, and together form a whole that defines the place of the Bhṛgus in the social and spiritual orders. They are, however, connected in two important ways. Both are concerned with the themes of death and the restoration of life; also, one major Bhārgava, Cyavana, figures significantly in both major portions of the cycle.

The relations of the Bhṛgus with the gods and demons, like their relations with the kṣatriyas, are characterized by a high degree of ambivalence. The Bhṛgus are shown as worshiping and assisting the various divinities of Brahmanism and Hinduism and as receiving from them in turn assistance, special favors, and boons. Yet the same sages are frequently shown as bitterly hostile to various gods, threatening and even cursing them, while they themselves are often the objects of the gods' wrath. The picture is further complicated by the fact that one of the Bhṛgus, Śukra, is the friend and minister of the asuras, the demon enemies of the gods, while, largely in postepic texts, another, Rāma, is said to be an incarnation of the supreme divinity.

The myths of the Bhṛgus and the gods are unlike those of the Bhṛgus and the kṣatriyas in two interesting respects. First, the former often have clear vedic antecedents, while preepic sources for the latter are vague at best and often wholly lacking. Second, the events of the former are frequently credited with having enduring effects observable in social, mythical, or even physical phenomena, while such effects are rare in the latter.

The Foes of Heaven

As in the case of the Bhṛgus' ambivalent relations to the kṣatriyas, it is hostility that emerges as the more characteristic phenomenon and the one that most clearly sets the group apart from the other famous sages and priestly families of Indian myth. Many of the important brahmanical lines are said to be descended from great ṛṣis, including Bhṛgu, who are offspring of the god Brahman. Moreover, stories of familiarity between the various sages, Bhārgava and non-Bhārgava, and the gods are numerous in the epics and the Purāṇas. But the motifs of hostility, violence, and curses between gods and sages, while occurring sporadically in other priestly myths, are virtually definitive of this portion of the Bhārgava cycle.[2]

The enmity of the Bhṛgus is not restricted to any one god or to any one type of god. They even occasionally turn against Viṣṇu and Śiva, the supreme deities of sectarian Hinduism, as well as against the lesser gods, the survivors of the vedic pantheon.

Viṣṇu and his various avatars are seldom the targets of Bhārgava wrath in the *Mahābhārata*. Even when they are, the episodes are dubious and of minor interest here. Of the two episodes in which Vaiṣṇava incarnations do appear to be in conflict with Bhṛgus, one, a bizarre encounter between Rāma Jāmadagnya and Rāma Dāśarathi, is a palpably late interpolation.[3] In the other, the sage Uttaṅka, angered by Kṛṣṇa's failure to prevent the Bhārata war, threatens to curse him.[4] However, when the sage realizes the true nature of Kṛṣṇa he is humbled and requests a vision of the god's cosmic form.[5] Thus the threat is not carried out and is, in any case, predicated on Uttaṅka's ignorance of Kṛṣṇa's divine nature. It is possible that this encounter is a creation modeled on other Bhārgava myths in which sages curse the gods.[6]

The relations between Viṣṇu and the Bhṛgus in the Purāṇas are considerably more complex and are illustrated by a large number of stories. These are, however, basically of sectarian rather than strictly Bhārgava interest and are, in any case, generally beyond the scope of this study.[7] However, the narrative of Śukra and the asuras (ŚA) which appears in the *Matsya* and other Purāṇas[8] provides, along with its many other variants of important Bhārgava material, a striking example of hostility directed toward Viṣṇu.

Bhṛgu's wife, the mother of Śukra, makes use of a magical spell to paralyze Indra, the king of the gods (ŚA 35). When Viṣṇu attempts to intervene to save him, he finds himself in similar straits through the woman's power and, in terror of her, manages to behead her (ŚA 40–43). Bhṛgu, angered at the god's act of self-defense, curses him to be born seven times among men (ŚA 45). This extraordinary curse is in fact fulfilled and is said to be responsible for the incarnations of Viṣṇu (SA 46,132–33).[9]

Śiva seems only once to be at odds with a Bhārgava in the *Mahābhārata*, where in one myth a state of the bitterest enmity is seen to have prevailed between Śukra and Śiva (ŚŚ).[10] Once again, as in the purāṇic story mentioned above, a great god attacks a Bhārgava in an attempt to protect another, lesser divinity (ŚŚ 9–13). The episode is obscure in a number of respects. However, it is clear that Śukra is able, by means of his extraordinary yogic powers, to withstand and partially frustrate the wrath of the supreme lord (ŚŚ 14–26). Only after ages of severe penances does Śiva appear to be able to muster the power to discomfit the sage (ŚŚ 22–29). Even so, the Bhārgava, though he is bested, manages to thwart the god's intention of killing him and even to emerge from the god's belly in the status of his son (ŚŚ 27–37).

Although Viṣṇu and Śiva, the great gods of sectarian Hinduism, are thus not wholly immune to Bhārgava wrath, it is the lesser gods, those whose cults declined in postvedic India, who are most frequently the objects of the Bhṛgus' enmity. They are repeatedly humbled before the power of the Bhṛgus.

Indra, chief of the postvedic pantheon, is the central victim of Bhārgava anger. He is humiliated and nearly destroyed in separate incidents by three of the Bhṛgus. The most important story involving such a humiliation is that of Indra's conflict with the sage Cyavana over the question of the admission of the Aśvins to the soma-sacrifice (C 60–83). In the course of this dispute the god is paralyzed, terrified, and all but destroyed through the power of the sage. In the end he is forced to capitulate ignominiously. The story is interesting for several reasons. It is perhaps the oldest attested Bhārgava myth in the sense that it has unmistakable and unambiguous vedic antecedents.[11] Moreover, the Cyavana episode is the one major Bhārgava myth in which the two themes of Bhṛgu-kṣatriya and Bhṛgu-god relations are linked. The story is a popular one and has exerted great fascination over the redactors of the epic,[12] who repeat it in various forms three times. It is thus second only to the career of the Bhārgava Rāma in the imagination of the Bhārgava mythmakers.

The motif of the paralysis and near destruction of Indra is a strange one, and it is therefore particularly interesting that it appears again in the *Matsyapurāṇa* version of the encounter of Indra with Bhṛgu's wife. In both cases the god, rushing to attack, is immobilized by the sorcery of the Bhṛgus (cf. C 59–60 and ŚA 33–36).

The king of the gods is thwarted again in the epic by the Bhārgava boy Vipula.[13] Here, too, a magical or yogic paralysis is employed to frustrate and humiliate the god, although in this instance it is inflicted not upon Indra but upon Ruci, the object of his lust.

Vipula is left to guard the chastity of Ruci, the wife of Devaśarman, his guru. Indra, true to his character, attempts to take advantage of Devaśarman's absence to seduce his wife. Vipula, however, takes yogic possession of Ruci and prevents her from responding to the advances of the lustful god. Indra becomes aware of the young sage's presence and becomes terrified lest he be cursed.[14] Vipula emerges from the body of Ruci and scolds the errant god.

> Unrestrained, wicked, lustful Indra! Neither men nor gods will long worship you. Have you forgotten Śakra, has it slipped your mind that when you were dismissed by Gautama you mere marked

> all over with cunts? I know you for a fool, one devoid of self-control and constancy. She is guarded by me. Go, wretch, as you have come, you fool. I will not burn you up this time with my inherent luster. I am moved by pity and do not wish to burn you, Vāsava.[15]

Finally, the frightened divinity is dismissed with the warning that he is lucky to escape with his life. Indra slinks away without a word.[16]

The motif of magical or yogic paralysis of a god occurs again in the Śāntiparvan narrative of the encounter of Śukra and Śiva. There it is Kubera, the god of wealth, who is the victim of Bhārgava aggression. This is the only myth in the epic in which a sage attacks a supernatural being for purely venal motives. Śukra enters and immobilizes Kubera, the lord of the yakṣas, in order to steal his vast wealth (ŚŚ 9), and this theft provokes the sage's protracted contest with Śiva. Moreover, despite the angry intervention of the great god, there is nothing in the passage to indicate that the Bhārgava is forced to return what he has stolen. With respect to the paralysis motif, this story, with its use of *parakāyapraveśa*, the yogic possession of another's body, appears to be closer to the Vipula story than to the encounters of Indra with Cyavana and Bhṛgu's wife.

Two other gods of some significance in the epic pantheon are likewise subject to curses and threats on the part of Bhārgava sages.

The fire-god Agni, the great sacrificial divinity of the Vedas, is said to have been cursed by Bhṛgu for having discharged his function as the ultimate *sākṣin*, witness, in a way unfavorable to the sage. This incident is related in the Paulomaparvan, a section of the Ādiparvan given over wholly to Bhārgava myths.[17] There it is said that the rakṣas Puloman, who abducted Bhṛgu's pregnant wife Pulomā, did so only after having consulted with

Agni as to whether the woman belonged by right to him or to the sage.[18] Agni realizes that the demon's claim is just and becomes dejected, fearful on the one hand of telling a lie and on the other of Bhṛgu's wrath.[19] Finally, the god, unable to utter a falsehood, advises the demon to take the woman. Puloman abducts her, only to be destroyed by the effulgent birth of her infant Cyavana.[20] When Bhṛgu learns of what has happened he demands to know who has betrayed his wife to the demon: "Tell the truth. In my anger I wish to curse him at once. Who would not fear my curse? Who has done this?"[21] When Pulomā names Agni as the informer, the sage carries out his threat and curses the god so that he becomes an eater of everything.[22] Agni then vows no longer to perform his function as the sacrificial fire, whereby the oblations are conveyed to the gods and the ancestors. The resultant chaos is stopped when the god Brahman grants Agni the boon that, though he must consume anything, whatever he touches will thereby be purified.[23]

Sūrya, the sun god, is also intimidated by a Bhārgava sage, in this case Jamadagni. The story is narrated in chapters 97 and 98 of the Anuśāsanaparvan and is of special interest because of its connection with the lineage of Aurva and its association with the dhanurveda. This is one of the few myths in the epic in which the sages of this lineage are involved significantly with the gods and virtually the only one in which hostility is expressed.

Reṇukā, engaged in the task of recovering the arrows fired by her husband in practice, momentarily rests in the shade of a tree to escape the heat of the sun which is afflicting her head and feet.[24] Jamadagni, as implacable as ever toward his wife, demands to know the reason for her delay. When he hears it he is enraged and prepares to shoot down the sun.[25] Sūrya appears, assuming the form of a brahman, and attempts to dissuade

Jamadagni. Failing in this, he must beg for his life.[26] Having thus humiliated the god, Jamadagni relents, and Sūrya gives him an umbrella and a pair of sandals to protect himself from the sun's heat. It is because of this incident, the narrative concludes, that giving these articles is meritorious.[27]

This concludes the list of individual gods who are subjected to the hostility and dominance of the Bhṛgus in the epic.[28] There are, however, a number of references to Bhārgava control or intimidation of the gods in general that are also worth mentioning. In the Āraṇyakaparvan version of the origin of the Bhārgava Rāma, Jamadagni is said to have brought the gods under his control (R 25). In the myth of Śukra and the asuras, the anger that Bhṛgu's wife unleashes upon Indra is also directed against the rest of the gods, who are following their leader into battle. When they see Indra reduced to helplessness they flee (ŚA 33–37). In the Anuśāsanaparvan version of the quarrel between Cyavana and Indra, Mada, the monster created by the sage, does not single out the chief of the gods for his attack, but begins to devour all the gods at once. "All the gods, along with Indra, were on the back of his tongue, like fish in the ocean finding themselves in the mouth of a whale."[29]

The hostility of most of the Bhṛgus for the gods is sporadic. The one Bhārgava who is systematically inimical to the gods has this characteristic as a function of his formal affiliation with the demon enemies of heaven. The association of the sage Śukra with the asuras is one of strangest peculiarities of the Bhārgava corpus. As such it will be treated separately below.

The myths of the encounters of the Bhṛgus and the gods, particularly those of hostile or ambivalent encounters, have one additional feature in common that serves to distinguish these myths from those involving the Bhṛgus and the kṣatriyas.[30] The great majority of these episodes serve to explain the origin of some particular phenomenon of social, religious, or even physical reality.[31] In fact it may be said that, aside from the magnification of Bhārgava prestige, one major purpose of the stories of Bhṛgu conflict with the gods is the explanation of such phenomena.

The encounter of Cyavana and Indra serves to explain two phenomena of different orders of reality. In the area of religion the story seeks to explain the participation of the Aśvins in the soma sacrifice of the gods.[32] In the area of social reality it explains, through Cyavana's apportionment of the demon Mada, "intoxication," the reason for men's infatuation with liquor, sex, gambling, and hunting (C 84). Bhṛgu's curse is said to account for no less significant a religious phenomenon than the incarnations of the lord Viṣṇu himself.[33] The same sage's curse of Agni is said to account for the fact that fire can consume anything, from the sacrificial oblations to corpses, without being defiled. Jamadagni's humiliation of Sūrya is the rationale for the merit involved in giving of umbrellas and sandals.

The obscure and inconclusive conflict between Śiva and Śukra is used to account for a number of phenomena, some of which are themselves relatively obscure. The episode is narrated by Bhīṣma in response to a series of questions concerning Śukra. Among these questions are one relating to how he came to be known as Śukra and another inquiring why he is unable to move through the air (ŚŚ 4–5). Both questions are explained by the fact of the Bhārgava's escape from Śiva's body through the god's penis (ŚŚ 32). He is called Śukra since he emerged through the same aperture as does semen (*śukra*). Why this should prevent the sage from moving through the air is not clear.[34] The incident also provides an extremely obscure etymology for the name of Śiva's trident, Pināka.[35] Even Indra's frustration at the hands of Vipula serves as an occasion to explain the decline of the god's cult in postvedic India.[36]

The Beloved of the Gods

If the Bhṛgus' relations with the gods are, like their associations with the princes, marked by a high degree of ambivalence, so, in both cases, do the positive aspects of these relations lack the dramatic impact of the negative. It is unquestionably the darker side of these relations that is distinctively Bhṛguid. Many sages and priestly families are said to have been on friendly and even intimate terms with the various divinities. Nonetheless, the less hostile associations of the various Bhṛgus and gods are of considerable significance to an understanding of this subcycle of myth.

The most intimate association of a Bhārgava sage with a god is that of Bhṛgu and the great god Brahman. The *Mahābhārata* shows awareness of a vedic tradition according to which Bhṛgu is the son of the god, born either from his heart or directly from his seed.[37] Yet aside from a few scattered references to this relationship, the epic contains no myths that demonstrate any particular intimacy between the two.[38] The closest thing to a functional filial relation between a god and a Bhṛgu in the mythic cycle is that which is established between Śiva and Śukra in the Śāntiparvan (ŚŚ 34–35). Although Śukra becomes the god's "son" only by extraordinary means and the relationship finds no genealogical support in the Vedas or in the epic, the special relationship between the two is confirmed by a number of purāṇic passages. Śiva is said to have rewarded the sage for his severe penance by instruction in the mṛtasaṃjīvinī vidyā and other extraordinary boons (ŚA 61–68).[39] The association between these two figures is thus perhaps somewhat more consistent than most of the others posited between the Bhārgavas and the gods.

The theme of a Bhṛgu as a disciple of Śiva occurs once more in the epic in a myth that is anomalous in the context of the special concerns of the Bhārgava cycle. The passage[40] attempts to explain the Bhārgava Rāma's mastery of the dhanurveda and his skill in the use of divine weaponry in terms of a boon of Śiva. It is said that at the request of Śiva, Rāma, although he was unskilled at arms,[41] undertakes to do battle against the asuras. He is assured that he will gain victory by meditating on Śiva. He does so and, having slain all the asuras, he receives the divine weapons that he wishes.[42]

This story is odd in a number of respects. It is the only place in the epic where Rāma is said to associate with the gods and, especially, to fight their battles with the asuras. Moreover, its account of Rāma's acquisition of the dhanurveda is in direct contradiction to a central, crucial, and well-established Bhārgava tradition.[43] Thus the episode cannot really be said to belong to the tradition of the Bhārgavas and the gods, except insofar as it plays upon that theme for other purposes.[44]

A number of the Bhṛgus are said in the epic to have enjoyed special relationships to Viṣṇu in his several forms and incarnations. The great Bhārgava sage Mārkaṇḍeya survives the cosmic dissolution and has an interesting encounter with the god as Nārāyaṇa in the form of a child.[45] Likewise, Uttaṅka, having first threatened Kṛṣṇa, is granted a vision of the god's divine form.[46] Perhaps the most curious of all the associations the Bhṛgus have with Viṣṇu is the identification of Rāma Jāmadagnya as an incarnation. This identification, however, is mainly a feature of the Purāṇas and is probably not known to the oldest version of the *Mahābhārata* text.[47]

Among the minor divinities it is unquestionably the Aśvins whose association with a Bhārgava sage is the most provocative. The association is an old one, known to the seers of the *Ṛgveda*. It is also of mutual benefit in that the gods are able to restore the sage's youth and he, in turn, is able to gain admittance for them to the sacrificial session of the gods. This myth appears to be the only one in the literature in which a sage performs such a feat.[48] In effect, according to the epic versions at least, Cyavana has created new gods by forcing Indra and the rest of the pantheon to share the sacrifice with upstarts condemned by the king of the gods on the grounds that they are lowly servants and physicians who associate with men (C 61–64). The myth may contain a reminiscence of Bhārgava association with cults that were assimilated relatively late into the vedic religion.

Other, more minor references to close relationships between the Bhṛgus and the gods occur in episodes in which Brahman divulges knowledge of the future to Śukra and Cyavana (ŚA 112–22, CK 11) and in which Ṛcīka has recourse to Varuṇa when he is in need of special horses to pay the bride-price of Satyavatī (R 9–11).[49]

Śukra, the Priest of the Demons

The encounters of the Bhṛgus with the gods are mostly of an irregular character. In very few cases do particular Bhṛgus have special relationships with individual gods which persist throughout the cycle. Thus, for example, in one myth Rāma may be said to have a special relationship to Śiva, in another to Viṣṇu, while for the most part he has no particular connection with any of the gods. Uśanas Kāvya, or Śukra, however, is an important exception to this rule. Throughout the literature of the epic and purāṇic periods, Śukra is regularly associated with Śiva and is consistently identified as the purohita of the asuras. As such he is the counterpart and arch-rival of the Āṅgirasa priest Bṛhaspati[50] and the only Bhārgava to be a foe of the gods by profession.

The relationship between Śukra and the asuras is one of the most provocative and puzzling aspects of Bhārgava myth. That

Bhṛgus should show hostility for the gods on some occasions is strange, but that one of the greatest of the Bhārgava sages should regularly champion the asuras, the forces of chaos and evil—in short, of adharma—against the divine personifications of dharma is perplexing and has no non-Bhārgava parallel in the literature. The origin of the relationship was evidently puzzling to the epic redactors themselves, for the question is raised at least twice in the *Mahābhārata*. In neither case is the answer given wholly satisfying.

The issue is raised most explicitly by Yudhiṣṭhira in the prologue to the encounter of Śukra and Śiva. The Pāṇḍava prince asks Bhīṣma why the sage became a partisan of the demons and hostile to the gods (ŚŚ 2–3). Bhīṣma's reply is uncharacteristically brief. He says that Śukra sided with the demons out of pity (ŚŚ 7).[51] The great Kaurava then proceeds immediately with his story of Śukra, Kubera, and Śiva, a story that makes no reference whatever to the asuras but that seems to presuppose the Bhārgava's hostility for the gods.[52] Another important epic myth concerning Śukra traces his partisanship to the endless struggle between the gods and the demons for control of the universe (ŚK 5–6). However, it is simply stated that the gods chose Bṛhaspati as their purohita, while the demons had recourse to Śukra. No reasons for the choice or the sage's acceptance are provided. Evidently the epic bards are either unsure of the answer or not interested in the question.

Whatever the reason for Śukra's acceptance of his unusual post as spiritual adviser to the enemies of the gods, his conduct in that position is of great interest. Unlike his rival's association with the gods, Śukra's tenure as the asuras' purohita is dramatic, turbulent, and often highly emotional. Several sources suggest that in wisdom and sheer mastery of brahmanical powers, the Bhārgava is superior even to Bṛhaspati. For he possesses the miraculous mṛtasaṃjīvinī vidyā of which the Āṅgirasa is wholly ignorant

(ŚK 7–9, ŚA 21). It is frequently made clear that the gods are fearful of him and have been made to suffer at his hands (ŚK 10–11, ŚA 10, ŚŚ 3). He is said to have acquired his enormous power through penances that none other had ever accomplished (ŚA 62–63).

Śukra's major function in the mythology is to use his wisdom and great power in the service of the asuras in their continuing battle with the gods. He is able to restore to life the demons slain by the gods, while Bṛhaspati is helpless to do this for his patrons. He undergoes the severest possible austerities for their sake. When, despite his efforts, the asuras lack the strength necessary to attack or withstand the gods, he advises them with wisdom and cunning so that they may avoid open conflict until they are ready (ŚA 11–19).

Despite the evident advantages of having such an ally, the asuras are, as always in Indian mythology, ultimately defeated. Their defeat results partially from their own foolishness (ŚK 39, ŚA 88–100), which leads them to disregard Śukra, and partially from the gods' cunning in circumventing Śukra's plans (ŚK 10–13, ŚA 54–56, 81–84).

In addition to these reasons, there is the fact that Śukra, true to his characterization in the Vedas, shows a decided ambivalence in his regard for his patrons. Against his compassion, affection, and loyalty[53] may be set his recurrent anger, disaffection, and betrayal. In the long and complex saga of Śukra and the asuras, Śukra is said to have twice abandoned the demons to their fate, and even to have cursed them (ŚA 1–3, 101–2, 108). Once he is moved to do so by his rage at their foolish rejection of him, but the first time he appears to be motivated simply by a desire to join the gods and assist at their sacrifice. Moreover, in the same episode, Śukra's two students, Śaṇḍa and Marka, who have taken their guru's place as purohitas of the demons, likewise allow themselves to be seduced by the gods' offer of a chance to participate in the sacrifice. Accordingly, they, too, abandon their charges (ŚA 129–31). In the myth of Śukra and Kaca, Śukra willingly takes on the son of his bitter rival as a pupil although he seems to know that the boy had come to gain the saṃjīvinī vidyā for the gods (ŚK 16–21). The asuras are keenly aware of the threat posed by Kaca's discipleship and act so as to thwart its purpose (ŚK 25–26,33). Śukra regards their actions as hostile to him and designed to make him lose his status as a brahman (ŚK 39). Finally, having passed the spell on to Kaca, the sage rebukes the demons sharply (ŚK 57).

Even Śukra's abandonment of the asuras is not decisive. In both instances of his abandoning them he is immediately thereafter moved by pity for their plight and returns to aid them once again[54] (ŚA 3–5, 111 ff.). Indeed, the Bhārgava seems unable to decide between the asuras and their foes on any consistent basis.[55]

One additional feature of the myths concerning Śukra and the asuras is of interest in the light of the myths in which the more direct relations of the Bhṛgus and the gods are described. Like these myths, the Śukra myths are concerned in part with explanations of social or natural phenomena. Alarmed by his heedless behavior while intoxicated, Śukra is credited with having originated the prohibition against the consumption of alcohol by brahmans (ŚK 53–55). This prohibition is of great significance in the brahmanical tradition and is still a vital issue for orthodox brahmans.

Observations

The relations between the Bhārgavas and the inhabitants of the supernatural realms are, like their associations with the earthly kṣatriyas, notable for their ambivalence. The hostility of the Bhṛgus for many of the gods of the epic pantheon is curious, as is the peculiar relationship between Śukra and the demon enemies of the gods. As with the kṣatriyas, Bhārgava relations with the gods, whether of an intimate or antipathetic nature, are more numerous and pronounced than are those of other brahman families. The myths expressive of these relations appear to form a separate subcycle of Bhārgava myth, of which the central figures are Uśanas Kāvya or Śukra and his family. This subcycle is the complement of that involving the kṣatriyas and centering around the descendants of Cyavana. The two together define virtually the whole of the Bhārgava corpus in the epic.

4
Masters of the Epic

The foregoing chapters are an attempt to dissect the main body of Bhārgava myth and to isolate its major repeated structural elements. Through this effort and through comparison of similar elements of theme and motif in different contexts, it has become possible to demonstrate that the cycle was developed in large measure through the isolation, borrowing, and manipulation of these elements.

In the light of this evidence it is now appropriate to attempt an evaluation of the entire cycle as it appears in the *Mahābhārata* in order to provide answers to some basic questions concerning these myths and their function in the great epic. Finally, it should be possible, on the basis of the content of the myths and the mythic cycle, to shed some light on problems of interpretation; to attempt to grasp the meaning of the strange and violent world of the Bhṛgus.

The Cycle

One of the most striking features of the Bhārgava material in the *Mahābhārata*, aside from the obviously dramatic nature of the myths themselves, is its structure. Bhārgava myth is marked by two major binary oppositions that by their intersection establish four subareas into which virtually all the submythic elements fall.

First, the cycle itself is divisible into two largely separate and complementary portions, one dealing with the kṣatriyas and the other with the gods and other supernatural beings. The first of these subcycles deals mainly with the figures of Cyavana, Aurva, and Rāma, while the second is centrally concerned with the deeds of Cyavana and Śukra. Next, each of these subcycles is itself divided into two opposing modes, owing to the thoroughgoing ambivalence that characterizes the relations between the Bhṛgus and both groups. These modes reflect the positive and negative, the amicable and hostile or "love" and "hate" facets of Bhārgava myth.

Thus the great bulk of the mythic elements, including virtually all those significant enough to be repeated in more than one episode or in connection with more than one Bhṛgu sage, fall easily into one of the four following quadrants: hate/kṣatriyas, love/kṣatriyas, hate/gods, and love/gods. In addition, the cycle is much concerned with the binary distinction of life/death. This is only partially to be superimposed on the love/hate alternation and may be considered as at least a partially independent factor.[1]

This simple quadripartite division of submythic elements into modal variants of the subcycles points up a crucial feature of the Bhārgava myths. Many of the major myths, and especially those concerning the three most important Bhārgavas, Śukra, Cyavana, and Rāma, are complex. They consist of several plots related in sequence or interwoven. Thus the myth of Cyavana consists of the episodes of Sukanyā and of Indra bound loosely together through the motif of the Aśvins and Śaryāti's sacrifice.

The myth of Śukra and Kaca interweaves the battle between the gods and the demons, and the struggle for the life-giving magic, with the romance of Kaca and Devayāni. The elaborate versions of the origins and career of the Bhārgava Rāma present in chronological sequence a number of related incidents extending over at least three generations. In each case these myths contain at least one element from each of the four quadrants. Thus the Rāma complex, essentially concerned with hate/kṣatriya and death elements, manages to incorporate not only modally related love/kṣatriya themes in the marriages of Ṛcīka and Jamadagni, but the seemingly unrelated themes of love/gods and hate/gods. Even the motif of restored life is included. Similarly, the sequel to the episode of Śukra and Kaca, the story of Yayāti, is itself a major treatment of the Bhṛgu/kṣatriya issue. In several such cases it is apparent that the relatively extraneous elements have been brought in deliberately, and it seems likely that the purpose of such borrowings (for the elements are most often taken from some obvious source, Bhārgava or non-Bhārgava) is to make each of the major myths representative of the scope of the entire cycle.

The myths in which this process of incorporation is most pronounced, exhibit in its clearest form the extraordinary degree of interdependence that distinguishes the cycle from most of the non-Bhṛguid mythology of the epic literature. The three figures, Cyavana, Śukra, and Rāma, thus form the Bhārgava cycle's nexes, around which the greatest number of episodes and thematic elements have clustered in the *Mahābhārata*. Moreover, their power and fascination is such that their appearances are not confined to any one myth.

Rāma and Cyavana each appear in a central myth that attests to their stature and defines their functions. Rāma's function is the slaughter of the warrior class and the presentation of the earth as a gift to the brahmans. Cyavana's is his rejuvenation and his championship of the Aśvins. Both myths are well developed in the epic and are represented by numerous widely dispersed variants in the *Mahābhārata* and the Purāṇas. Yet the significance of these myths and of their heroes is such that both Rāma and Cyavana have grown in the imaginations of the epic poets beyond the confines of their proper myths. Thus Rāma appears as the teacher and counsellor of several of the kṣatriya heroes of the *Mahābhārata* and occasionally is to be found taking an active role in the epic itself despite the fact that the events of his proper myth are thought to have occurred in an age long before that of the Bhārata war. Similarly, the stature of Cyavana is such that the Bhārgava redactors choose him to serve as the representative and spokesman of the clan in the Kuśika episode of the Anuśāsanaparvan, while in the same book he is the central figure in a curious story concerning the king Nahuṣa and the Bhārgava's extreme affection for a school of fish.[2]

Unlike Rāma and Cyavana, Śukra does not appear in the epic as the hero of any single definitive myth that is repeated or varied throughout the poem. Instead he appears in a number of myths which do, however, vary and reiterate the sage's basic role as the minister of the asuras and his ambivalent but essentially hostile relationship to the gods. In addition, his career appears to serve as the central locus of the motif of the restoration of the dead. Although it is in part this very catholicity, this eclecticism drawing from all the quadrants of the corpus, that defines these three Bhārgavas as central, by no means do their myths represent the different areas of Bhārgava concern equally. An examination of the distribution of Bhārgava themes and motifs among the myths of these figures based on the conspectus of Bhārgava myth given in the preceding chapters is of the greatest interest in this regard and sheds light on the structure and significance of the entire corpus of Bhṛguid myth in the *Mahābhārata.* From the point of view of the pervasive themes of the clan's relations with the kṣatriyas and the gods, the three figures, Rāma, Śukra, and Cyavana and their myths show a very marked distribution and present, as a group, a curious symmetry.

As we have seen, the Aurva-Rāma subcycle is concerned virtually to the point of obsession with the stormy relations of that branch of the Bhārgavas with the kṣatriyas. Its few and sketchy references to the contact of the Bhṛgus with the gods and other supernatural beings are in no way seriously involved with this central concern. Rather they often appear as afterthoughts and are sometimes wholly senseless.[3] Indeed, it would appear that the major rationale for these references is the recognition of them as representative of a crucial Bhārgava concern and a consequent desire on the part of the redactors to lend a sort of legitimacy, a pan-Bhārgava appeal to the subcycle.

The Śukra myths are similarly monovalent and complement the Aurva-Rāma myths, for Śukra is involved almost exclusively with supernatural beings and forces. Even where the Śukra subcycle does deal with the relations of the brahmans and the kṣatriyas, the issue is thrashed out not with a human king but with the king of the asuras.[4]

Unlike these two Bhārgavas, Cyavana is truly and significantly bivalent, representing in his central myth both the major Bhṛguid concerns. He is the champion of the Aśvins and the classic foe of Indra and the gods, and he is also the kinsman and priest of the Mānava line of kings and the would-be annihilator of the Kauśikas. Thus while Rāma and Śukra represent the social and spiritual poles respectively of Bhārgava affect, Cyavana seems to represent both. His central myth appears to bridge the gap between these two critical areas and thus serves as the only major Bhārgava myth to represent fully all the important issues of the corpus.

An examination of the three central myths with regard to their distribution of Bhārgava motifs is similarly illuminating. The central myth of Cyavana, in keeping with its general catholicity, is a repository of recurrent motifs that appear as natural components of the complex story spanning all the cycle's quadrants. Thus for example it contains the motif of the innocent ascetic outraged by and avenged upon the kṣatriyas and the motif of the immobilization of the king of the gods. Moreover a number of motifs associated with the myth and with its pre-epic variants have interesting connections with material in other Bhārgava and Bhārgava-related myths. Examples of these are the motif of the sole survivor[5] (and also the self-destructive grief of Cyavana and Vasiṣṭha) and the sexual rejuvenation of the senile. The myths of Śukra are much more parochial in their motifs than those of Cyavana. Not only do they restrict themselves thematically to one area of the Bhārgava cycle, but they more consistently use motifs that do not recur in other portions of the cycle. This is seen especially in connection with such motifs as the second birth from another's body and the defection of the purohita(s). Even those motifs that appear elsewhere in the cycle, such as the beheading of the mother and the spell for restoring the dead, seem clearly to be more integral to the Śukra myths. Only in the case of the paralysis of a god or gods is it likely that the motif may have been borrowed from Cyavana's subcycle.

In contrast to these two subcycles with their limited number of recurrent motifs, the Aurva-Rama subcycle is a veritable storehouse of Bhārgava material. In the Aurva episode it is clear that several important motifs, such as universal destruction and genocide, are closely related to motifs in the framing Vāsiṣṭha complex. Nonetheless, its use of the motif of genocidal revenge in the Bhārgava episode of Ruru and in the epic account of Janamejaya's genocidal snake sacrifice make its original provenance uncertain. The Aurva episode's motifs of the sole survivor of the race and the effulgent embryo are paralleled almost exactly in the epic and earlier legends of Cyavana and are almost certainly of Bhṛguid origin.

The motif of marriage to the kṣatriyas occurs twice in this subcycle, with reference to Ṛcīka and Jamadagni. The incident of the switched boons, while functioning equally in the Kauśika cycle, is probably essentially a Bhārgava innovation.

The career of Rāma himself is, moreover, almost wholly a pastiche of motifs drawn from other portions of the subcycle, the cycle, and even non-Bhārgava myth. The motif of the cursed sons may belong properly to the Kauśika cycle.[6] Like the motifs of mother-murder and the restoration of life, which are obviously drawn from the Śukra complex, to which they are basic, this motif appears to have no function in the episode other than, perhaps, to establish its Bhārgava credentials.

The motif of the abduction of the calf is manifestly a borrowing from the story of Vasiṣṭha and Viśvāmitra, while the remaining motifs, especially those of the murder of Bhārgava priests by the Haihaya kṣatriyas, the genocidal campaign of a single archer, and the intervention of the departed ancestors, are all closely paralleled by material in the Aurvopākhyāna and the story of Pratardana and Vītahavya. In short, there scarcely seems to be a single important motif in the Rāma complex that is not to be found elsewhere in the Bhārgava cycle, or in one of the two other epic cycles with which it is closely involved. Moreover, wherever the original provenance of a given motif can be established by the contextual evidence it invariably appears that the Rāma myth has the motif at second hand. So although all three of the major Bhṛguid subcycles contain themes and materials common to the whole cycle, only the Rāma complex appears to be the original source of none of them.

This peculiarity of the Rāma myth is illuminated, at least in part, by yet another important distinction that sets it apart from the proper myths of Śukra and Cyavana. The latter two figures are both known to the *Ṛgveda*, while clear antecedents of their epic myths are elaborated in the literature of the Brāhmaṇa period. Cyavana's quarrel with the clan of Śaryāta, his restoration to youth at the hands of the Aśvins, his marriage to Sukanyā, his introduction of the Aśvins to the soma sacrifice, and even his humiliation of Indra by the creation of Mada are set forth in detail in the *Śatapatha Bhāhmaṇa* (IV.1.5.10 ff.) and *Jaiminīya Brāhmaṇa* (III.159–61). Similarly, Uśanas Kāvya is a figure of some significance in the *Ṛgveda* as a protegé and helper of Indra,[7] while his function as the powerful but inconstant priest of the asuras is firmly established in the later vedic literature.[8] In contrast, the vedic literature appears to know nothing whatever of the Bhārgava Rāma, nor does it contain any myth that might be viewed as the prototype of his central feat, the extermination of the kṣatriyas.[9]

Since the Rāma myth does not appear to predate the epic, and is almost wholly composed of elements from Bhārgava and other myths, many of which are traceable to the Vedas, it is impossible to avoid the conclusion that the myth itself is a deliberate creation of the epic bards intended to incorporate, in one complex, almost every highly charged feature of the Bhṛguid cycle.

On the basis of the evidence, therefore, the relationship of the three central Bhārgava complexes can be seen in two rather different lights, both of which, however, are illuminating. First, from a historical viewpoint, the affiliation of the myths may be described as follows. The Śukra and Cyavana complexes both have well-established and apparently independent sources in the Veda.[10] The Rāma complex must then be seen as in large part an extrapolation of elements developed from the older complexes. The Cyavana and Śukra subcycles can thus be regarded as "parent myths" with respect to the Rāma myth and, indeed, the whole cycle.

Second, a synchronic examination of the three mythic complexes establishes their structural relationship in the context of the Bhārgava cycle. The bivalence of the Cyavana myths, pertaining as they do equally to the gods and the kṣatriyas, establishes this sage as a mediating figure linking the other two complexes, each of which is centrally concerned with only one aspect of the cycle. In this way, Cyavana has managed to retain a good deal of vitality as a figure of epic and even purāṇic myth.[11] His is the mythic complex which in fact defines the basic concerns of the Bhārgavas in the *Mahābhārata*.

The significance of the Cyavana complex, the interweaving of the social and spiritual attitudes of the Bhṛgus, is clearly recognized by the Bhṛguid redactors of the epic. Surely the choice of this figure as the Bhārgavas' spokesman in the Cyavanakuśikasaṃvāda cannot be regarded as random. For here the sage's role of progenitor of the Aurva-Rāma line is amplified to make him, in addition, the editor and redactor of the myths of the entire sub-cycle. Cyavana is the only Bhṛgu who is himself a purveyor of Bhṛguid mythology. He becomes at once a model and an inspiration for the whole cycle and the mythic personification of the mythmakers themselves. To a great extent the cycle begins with Cyavana (and Śukra), the source of the central Bhārgava themes, and culminates with Rāma, in whose myth are gathered virtually all the Bhārgava motifs.

The Epic

The culmination of the epic Bhārgava cycle is undeniably the myth of Rāma Jāmadagnya. This is made abundantly clear both on structural grounds and because of the unparalleled popularity of the myth with the epic redactors. Further, a diachronic analysis of the corpus shows that the episode is the special invention of the epic. Yet the significance of this phenomena has been only partially understood.

In "The Bhṛgus and the Bhārata: a Text-Historical Study," Sukthankar showed conclusively that the epic as it has come down to us is to a great extent under the influence of the Bhṛgus. In several cases he discovered alterations and interpolations that could have no other explanation.[12] Yet the question of the significance of the Rāma myth remains unanswered in his work. In order to attempt to provide such an answer it is necessary to view the Rāma myth in two contexts, that of the Bhārgava cycle, and that of the *Mahābhārata* itself.

Although it is true that the Rāma myth contains little that is original in the way of themes and motifs, its configuration of its inherited elements is in one particular unique. For it has dramatically inverted the motif of the switch of varṇa-functions, typically concerned with the change from kṣatriya to brahman. The resultant character has been superimposed on the old figure of the vengeful brahman paying back the iniquities of the princes.[13] The result has been to create a spectacular figure, virtually unparalleled in the literature, the bloodthirsty brahman-warrior who has captured the imagination of the epic bards and of generations of Indians.

The reasons for this innovation, and for the fact that Rāma has all but supplanted figures like Aurva in the minds of the epic mythmakers, are closely bound up with the nature and functions of the epic itself. For regardless of how one imagines the evolution of the massive *Mahābhārata* out of the epic saga of the Kauravas and the Pāṇḍavas, it is clear that the original interest in the poem, and indeed a central concern even in the conflated epic, is the loves and wars of the princes of ancient India.[14] Yet it is also clear that the great epic, in its inherited form, is also the great encyclopedia of brahmanical civilization. It is a huge treatise on dharma in all its various applications; law, religion, philosophy, the social system, and so on. Moreover, though at heart it is a tale of chivalry and war, it consistently and emphatically asserts the superiority of the brahmans over the princely class.

Now, as Sukthankar has demonstrated, this brahmanic material, not directly germane to the epic story, shows the greatest degree of "bhṛguization." It is hardly surprising, then, that the one Bhṛgu especially created by the epic redactors should in some way personify the shift in the provenance of the poem from the hands of the *sūtas*, the bards and panegyrists of the princely courts, to those of its new custodians, the Bhṛgus.

In this light the extraordinary ferocity of Rāma and his family's peculiar predilection for the dhanurveda become clear. It was not enough for the Bhārgavas that their hero be superior to the kṣatriyas, even that he intimidate and finally destroy them. This much is asserted of many brahmans in the epic. Sages like Vasiṣṭha and Kaśyapa and, in the Bhṛguid tradition itself, Cyavana and especially Aurva had always stood as proof of the fearsome might of brahmanical *tapas*, the power of austerity. Yet the very ubiquity of such figures serves to weaken the power of the theme. Aurva is, after all, not sufficiently distinguishable from Parāśara to serve the Bhṛgus' purpose.

Moreover, in the light of the issue of the provenance of the original epic, the power of tapas alone is not enough: to mark the epic's passage out of the control of the kṣatriyas, Rāma must humiliate and even annihilate them with their own weapons. He must not only put them in their place, he must, by clearing the earth of them and their heirs, usurp that place. Even the great kṣatriya heroes of the Bhārata war must be shown as having obtained what skill at arms they have either directly or ultimately from the terrible Bhārgava. In taking the earth from the kṣatriyas Rāma fulfills his purpose, or rather the purpose of the Bhṛguid redactors.[15] In reality, it is not the earth or worldly sovereignty that the Bhṛgus or the brahmans ever took from the princes, but rather the control of the past, and with it the authoritative vehicle for social, moral, and spiritual dogma, the *Mahābhārata* itself.

Thus it is neither accident nor inane redundancy that makes Rāma's slaughter of the kṣatriyas crop up again and again in the course of the epic story and its mythological and legendary background. By this repetition the redactors are able to keep the feat and its significance constantly before the audience of the poem. Thus the formula *triḥsaptakṛtvaḥ* ("twenty-one times . . .") becomes a sort of trademark, stamped across the face of the vast epic to mark it as the product and possession of the Bhṛgus. Through Rāma's mythical extermination of the warrior class, the Bhārgavas have proclaimed themselves the masters of the epic.

The Bhṛgus

The discovery of the etiology of the Rāma mythos, and of its function in the Bhārgava cycle and in the epic as a whole, is of considerable importance from the standpoint of Indian mythological epic studies. Yet it does not deal with a basic area of interest, the actual content of the Bhārgava myths. Even though analysis shows that the Rāma story is a pastiche of Bhārgava motifs and themes, it does not explain the significance of these elements that are so persistently in the minds of the authors and editors of the various portions of the cycle. It is an understanding of these elements, if anything, that will provide the basis for answering the fascinating questions of the origins, history, and identity of the Bhṛgus. If such an analysis cannot provide a full answer to these questions, it may at least shed some light on possibly fruitful areas of inquiry.

The themes of the myths, the relations and actions in which the Bhṛgus are so constantly involved, are extraordinary. Virtually all of them are to some degree out of keeping with the traditions of brahmanical orthodoxy, if not explicitly prohibited by the Dharmaśāstra. The irony of this is heightened by the fact that the *Mahābhārata* itself is the great treatise on dharma, while the Bhṛgus are closely associated with the science of the law.[16]

Rāma is guilty of *strīhatyā*, the murder of a woman, a crime surely aggravated by its being, in his case, an act of matricide. Śukra, in his assault on Kubera, is guilty of theft and, until his unconscious ingestion of Kaca, is a drinker of liquor. His drunken lapse renders the sage an unwitting accomplice of the asuras in the greatest of crimes, *brahmahatyā*, the murder of a brahman. All these acts are strongly proscribed in the Smṛti literature, the first as an *upapātaka* or sin of the second degree, the rest as three of the dreaded *mahāpātakas*, the cardinal sins of brahmanical India.[17] All these acts are especially prohibited in the case of brahmans.

In addition, Rāma violates the varṇāśramadharma by taking up the violent career of a warrior, while all his ancestors by marrying princesses bring about *varṇasaṃkara*, the mixing of social classes that is so abhorrent to the brahmanical texts.[18] Yet even this does not exhaust the unorthodoxy of the Bhṛgus. Four of them, Cyavana, Śukra, Śukra's mother, and Vipula, use sorcery or yogic power in order to attack and humiliate the gods of the Hindu pantheon. Peculiar magical practices are used by Śukra and Bhṛgu for the miraculous resurrection of the dead, while Cyavana employs such means to conjure up a demon.[19] The same sage brings about a change in the very character of the vedic pantheon by forcing the admission of the Aśvins. Finally, and most provocatively, Śukra, often considered the greatest of Bhṛgu sages, is the household priest of the demons. Such behavior sets the Bhṛgus markedly apart from the other brahman clans of the epic.

Of the many peculiarities of this strange group, the ambivalence and violence of their relations with the kṣatriyas has attracted the greatest scholarly interest. This aspect of the cycle, the Aurva-Rāma tradition, is, for reasons discussed above, the more dynamic, and for the Bhṛgus themselves the more important, of the subcycles. As such and because of its potential value as a historical source, it has been subjected to more and closer scrutiny than the other aspects of the cycle.

In fact, it might be said that the first scholars to show interest in the Aurva-Rāma subcycle were the Bhṛgus. Clearly the Cyavanakuśikasaṃvāda is an effort to interpret the career of Rāma in the light of its connections with the Aurva episode and to explain the whole complex in terms of the Bhārgava's turbulent association with the kṣatriyas. More modern scholars have accepted Cyavana's synthesis in large measure and have used it as a basis for historical interpretations of the myths. Thus Karve felt that she had traced the history of the Bhārgava-Haihaya conflict from the days of Aurva down to those of Rāma and beyond.[20] Weller decided that "what has been traditionally handed down to us about the Bhṛguids in our *Mahābhārata* contains undoubtedly historical reminiscences," and that "the oft-repeated legend of Paraśu Rāma, who exterminated all warriors (Kṣatriyas) is evidence of a real tragic conflict in a hoary past."[21] Similarly, Charpentier decided that "perhaps historical happenings" form the basis of the Rāma story.[22]

In a sense these statements are correct. The Rāma complex is the culmination of a tradition of Bhārgava-kṣatriya ambivalence that dates to the vedic period. The epic complex may be traced to a vedic tradition of Cyavana as the sacrificial priest for the Śāryāta line of princes and as husband of the king's daughter. The identification of the Haihayas and Tālajaṅghas as branches of this line is thus fully in keeping with the tradition.[23] The historical reminiscences preserved in the Rāma complex most likely relate to a close affiliation between the Śāryāta-Haihaya line and the Bhṛgus, dating perhaps to the earliest Aryan civilization of the subcontinent.

The precise nature of this affiliation is far from clear, since the nature of the Bhṛgus themselves is in doubt. However, the claims of some scholars that the myths reflect, even in exaggerated form, an actual history of genocidal violence seem improbable. Whether, like Weller, one concludes that the Bhṛgus were the "primeval race" of India, the inhabitants of Mohenjo Daro, who under the leadership of Rāma staged a campaign for social and legal equality with the Aryans,[24] or, like Charpentier, that they actually drove some foreigners from their shores,[25] one is basing one's conclusion on impossible grounds. For although the Rāma story itself may contain some supporting elements, its history shows it clearly to be a fabrication of the epic redactors, crucial to an understanding of the Bhārgava cycle and even of the *Mahābhārata*, but actually of less historical value than any other Bhṛguid myth.

The Rāma complex is the end result not of a real war or campaign of genocide, but of a mythic tradition of Bhārgava-kṣatriya tension, centering around a struggle for status and a strong uncertainty as to the proper varṇa of the Bhṛgus. Thus the Bhārgava sages assert the brahmanical prerogatives by means of the weapons of the warrior.

Therefore, it seems more probable to speculate that in the Rāma complex, if not in fact the whole kṣatriya subcycle of the Bhārgava corpus, is preserved a mythic record of the earliest attested case of sanskritization in India. It may well be that the kṣatravṛttir brāhmaṇaḥ Rāma can be explained in the same way as his counterpart Viśvāmitra, as a mythic projection of either the elevation of a kṣatriya caste or the incorporation of a non-Aryan (or nonvedic) clan into the fold of orthodox brahmanism. It is possible that the Bhṛgus, a caste or clan who were masters of martial activities and possessed customs prohibited to orthodox brahmans, entered the ranks of a dominant or orthodox tradition, and that some of their abandoned practices might be preserved in their myths. In this way, Śukra's renunciation of liquor and his prohibition on its future use by brahmans might be viewed as a real reminiscence of an alteration in the practices of the group. The Bhārgava myth most unambiguously supporting such a hypothesis would not be the myth of Rāma, but rather that of Vītahavya, the kṣatriya who is elevated to the status of a Bhṛgu brahman. The epic tradition views both the Rāma and Vītahavya myths as myths of the same sort as that of Viśvāmitra, which would appear to involve just this sort of sanskritization.

Such a hypothesis, although open to many questions, has several advantages over those offered by previous scholars. In the first place, it is the only one that takes into consideration the textual history of the Rāma complex and its function in the Bhārgava cycle. Also, it would explain the ambivalence and the intermarriage between the Bhṛgus and the kṣatriyas, points that strictly historical interpretations tend to ignore. Finally, it provides a credible explanation for the fascination that the Kauśika myth of Viśvāmitra exerted over the Bhṛguid redactors of the Rāma myth.

The other aspect of Bhārgava myth, the strange relations between the Bhṛgus and the gods, although it has not proven so popular with scholars, is equally in need of explanation. For just as the Aurva-Rāma subcycle may provide clues as to the sociopolitical reality behind the Bhārgava cycle, so may the supernatural affairs of Cyavana and Śukra give us some insight into the socioreligious background of the myths.

The association of Cyavana with the Aśvins and the sage's hostile encounter with Indra for their sake is particularly suggestive. The sage is known as a protegé of the twin divinities in the *Ṛgveda* but it is not until the Brāhmaṇas that the nature of their relationship is made clear. In the *Śatapatha Brāhmaṇa*, Cyavana tells his benefactors that the sacrifice of the gods is headless and incomplete.[26] Through the wisdom of the sage, the Aśvins are able to teach the gods the head of the sacrifice and so become entitled to their share. In the *Jaiminīya Brāhmaṇa*, Cyavana himself offers the Aśvins' ladle, thus precipitating the quarrel between the Bhṛgus and the gods.[27] The point of both passages is the explanation of the origin of the offerings to the Aśvins, which are thus inextricably bound up with the Bhṛgus.[28]

The Bhārgava redactors of the epic amplify this episode considerably. In their versions Indra explicitly objects to the inclusion of the Aśvins on the grounds that they are not fit members of the pantheon, and he accedes only under duress. The myth has every appearance of representing a socioreligious event of some significance. It would appear that the Aśvins, the supernatural benefactors of Cyavana, might be the special divinities of a clan. If that clan or group were to be sanskritized or brought into the brahmanical fold at an early date, they might conceivably bring their own gods with them into the pantheon. If this were attempted, the orthodox priests might be expected to offer just such objections as are put into the mouth of Indra. Yet, if the sanskritized group were powerful and influential enough, perhaps associated closely with a newly powerful ruling group or family, there is every reason to believe that they might be successful.

Such an analysis of the Cyavana myth is, of course, premature. Yet it is a starting point and tends to reinforce rather than conflict with my speculation about the Bhārgava-kṣatriya subcycle.

Many of the remaining myths of the subcycle involving the gods serve mostly to magnify the greatness of the Bhṛgu sages in the *Mahābhārata*. They are thus an outgrowth of the Bhṛgu appropriation of the Bhārata epic and provide no great help in establishing the identity or history of the group.[29]

On the other hand, the identification of Śukra as the purohita and protector of the asuras is of great interest and may shed light on some of the most basic problems of early Indian and even early Indo-Iranian religion. If, as has been often suggested on the basis of the Iranian evidence, the asuras were the divinities of Aryans for whom, perhaps, the devas were demons, then Śukra and perhaps the Bhārgavas were originally their priests.[30] However, the problem of the asuras and an asura cult is by no means this simple and a fuller understanding of it, and of Śukra's role in it, awaits further research.[31] Still, the repeated theme of Śukra's and his disciples' ultimate disillusionment with the demons and their going over to the side of the gods may also be viewed as suggestive of a process of absorption of this branch of the Bhṛgus into the ranks of the orthodox brahmans.

The myths of Śukra are suggestive of still one more Bhṛguid affiliation that may shed some light on their history. This is the continued association of the Bhārgavas with the Āṅgirasas, another major brahmanical family of the mythological literature. By far the most important of the Āṅgirasas is Bṛhaspati, the purohita of the gods and the minister of Indra. From the point of view of the epic Bhārgava mythmakers, Bṛhaspati is of significance chiefly as the archrival of Śukra. Thus the Bhārgava protects the demons with his magical life-giving spell, which is unknown to the Āṅgirasa, and seeks such spells from Śiva. Kaca, the son of Bṛhaspati, in the role of Śukra's student, gets the spell for the gods, while in the *Matsyapurāṇa* saga of Śukra and the asuras Bṛhaspati himself impersonates the Bhārgava sage and so brings about the downfall of the asuras. In this latter incident the asuras seem not to care whether their guru is a Bhārgava or an Āṅgirasa (ŚA 99).

The association and even the possible confusion between the Bhārgavas and the Āṅgirasas is traceable to the Veda in contexts wholly unconcerned with Śukra. In the *Śatapatha Brāhmaṇa* version of the important Cyavana myth, the authors are unable to decide the affiliation of the sage. He is called "Cyavana the Bhārgava or the Āṅgirasa."[32] Moreover, the *Atharvaveda*, a text notoriously given over to spells, demonology, and black magic, is commonly referred to in the Atharvan literature as the Bhṛgvāṅgirasa, the Veda of the Bhṛgus and the Āṅgirasas.[33]

Finally, it is interesting to note that several of the most important feats of Bṛhaspati in the *Ṛgveda* are, in that text, also attributed to Uśanas Kāvya. Both figures are credited with having found out the secret name of the hidden cows and having either helped Indra to liberate them or to have freed them themselves.[34] This relationship, which seems to move from one of close association if not identification to one of sectarian rivalry, will bear further investigation. Such investigation may well contribute significantly to our understanding of the Bhṛgus and their role in ancient brahmanical literature.

A fuller understanding of the origins and role of the Bhṛgus clearly would be of paramount importance to an appreciation of the social, religious, and ethnic character of early Aryan civilization in India. This understanding will perhaps come when others of the groups with which they interact in the epic have themselves been subjected to closer scrutiny, and when, perhaps, new archaeological evidence has shed light on the obscure areas of vedic culture. Until such time, the Bhṛgus will have no monument but the strange and complex cycle of myths with which they sought to define themselves, and through which they molded to their own ends the greatest instrument of culture the Indian people have known.

Notes

Introduction

1. V. S. Sukthankar, "The Bhṛgus and the Bhārata: a Text-Historical Study," *ABORI* 18, pp. 1–76.

2. Ibid., p. 67.

3. Ibid., p. 70.

4. Ibid., p. 67–76.

5. Ibid., p. 2.

6. See R. P. Goldman, "Some Observations on the Paraśu of Paraśurāma," *JOIB* 21, no. 3 (1972), 153–65; idem., "Akṛtavraṇa vs. Śrīkṛṣṇa as Narrators of the Legend of Bhārgava Rāma *à propos* Some Observations of Dr. V. S. Sukthankar," *ABORI* 53 (1970), 161–73; Anujan Achan, "The Paraśurāma Legend and its Significance" (paper read at the eighth session of the All India Oriental Conference, Mysore, 1935); M. Biardeau, "La Décapitation de Reṇukā dans le Mythe de Paraśurāma," in *Pratidānam: Studies Presented to T.B.J. Kuiper* (The Hague: Mouton, 1969); S. S. Janaki, "Paraśurāma," *Puranam* 7 (1966), 52–82; I. Karve, "The Paraśurāma Myth," *JUB* 1 (1932), 115–39; and J. Charpentier, "Paraśurāma: the Main Outlines of his Legend," *Kuppuswami Shastri Commemoration Volume*, pp. 9–16.

7. Emil Sieg has written an excellent but limited article on the Bhṛgus in the Vedas. See article "Bhṛgu," in J. Hastings, ed., *The Encyclopedia of Religion and Ethics* (Edinburgh: T. T. Clark, 1959) p. 558.

8. In several Purāṇas and texts of the Mahātmya type, Reṇukā is identified with Devī, Jamadagni with Śiva, and Rāma as an avatāra of Viṣṇu. See especially the *SkP*, Sahyādrikhaṇḍa; the Kerala Mahātmya of the *Bhaviṣyapurāṇa*; Reṇukā Mahātmya; and *Brahmaṇḍ P* III.21–58. These stories, although occasionally based on an epic reference, are not known to the redactors of the *Mbh* and appear to be of rather later origin. See Sukthankar, "Bhṛgus and the Bhārata," p. 2; A. Bergaigne, *La Religion Vedique*, 4 vols. (2d ed., Paris: Librairie Honore Champion,

1963), I, 52–56; W. T. Elmore, "Dravidian Gods in Modern Hinduism: a Study of the Local and Village Deities of Southern India," *University Studies* (University of Nebraska) 15, no. 1, (1915), pp. 1–149.

9. In several vedic passages the Bhṛgus are identified as the sages who first brought fire to man. See *RV* I.60.1, II.4.2, X.46.2, III.50.10, X.46.9, I.58.6, II.24, etc. See also Sieg's article on the Bhṛgus in the Veda in Hastings, ed., *Encyclopedia of Religion and Ethics*,

10. E.g., Bhārgava Rāma as an avatār of Viṣṇu, and Bhṛgu used as the arbiter of the relative greatness of the three members of the Hindu trinity (*BhP* X.89).

11. Thus both episodes cited above are elaborated as Vaiṣṇava myth.

12. *Mahābhārata*: *Critical Edition*, V. S. Sukthankar, et. al., eds., 24 vols. with Harivaṃśa and Pratīka Index (Poona: Bhandarkar Oriental Research Institute, 1933–70).

13. The *Rām* is largely lacking in Bhārgava mythology. The main appearance of a Bhṛgu in that epic shows him in a very unfavorable light. See *Rām* 1.73–75. See also R. P. Goldman, "Vālmīki and the Bhṛgu Connection," JAOS 96, no. 1 (1976), 97–101.

14. In the *RV* there are 26 occurrences of the term *bhṛgu* (refer to Sieg's article on the Bhṛgus in the Veda, cited in note 7 above). Bhṛgu as the great sage of the later literature and as an eponymous ancestor of the Bhārgava clan is apparently unknown to the Ṛgvedic poets.

The term *bhṛgu* even when it occurs in the singular appears to be used collectively; see *RV* I.60.1, *RV* VIII.3.9, and *AV* V.19.1.

In the Brāhmaṇas the ṛṣi Bhṛgu is usually said to be of divine origin, springing either from the seed of Prajāpati (*ABr* III.33–34) or of Varuṇa (*PBr* 18.9.1 and *ŚBr* XI.6.1.1).

15. The five *mahāpāpas* or *mahāpātakas*, the great sins, are reckoned as (1) the slaying of a brahman (the greatest of sins), (2) consumption of alcoholic beverages, (3) major theft, (4) sexual relations with the wife of one's guru, and (5) association with any of these four. See *Manu* XI.54: *brahmahatyā surāpānaṃ steyam gurvaṅganāgamaḥ/mahānti pātakāny āhuḥ saṃsargaś cāpi taiḥ saha//Strīvadha*, woman-slaying, is not generally counted among the five great sins as enumerated in the law-texts. It is, in fact, reckoned among the *upapātakas* or lesser sins such as the slaying of a nonbrahman man (*Manu* XI.56). These are serious crimes, but not of the first magnitude.

16. Such an analysis of myths into separable and even interchangeable elements is not wholly unlike the techniques for the study of myth developed by Lévi-Strauss and his "structuralist school." Moreover, I would partially agree with Lévi-Strauss in his statement that, in regard to this type of analysis, "each gross constituent unit will consist in a relation." "The Structural Study of Myth" in Thomas A. Sebeok, ed., *Myth: A Symposium* (Bloomington: Indiana University

Press, 1955), pp. 86–87. We might not agree, however, as to what constitutes either a significant constituent element or a relation. In the case of the Bhārgava corpus, the greater part of the myths are focused on issues of establishing the relations of the Bhṛgus and their representatives to various non-Bhārgava groups. Indeed, the definition of the group in terms of hierarchical ranking may be said to be one of the central motives of the whole corpus. The definition of these relations is to be only partially compatible with Lévi-Strauss' identification of a relation as the predication of a function to a subject (ibid., p. 87). I might also note there that Lévi-Strauss's theory that a myth is the sum of all its versions is very poorly compatible with my intention to illuminate the corpus partly in terms of the significant contrastive features of its variants.

17. Exceptions were made for cow theft and role reversal, which recur in cycles of myth closely associated with the Bhārgava cycle by the Bhārgava redactors (e.g., the Vāsiṣṭha and Kauśika cycles).

18. Refer to CK and discussion in chapter 2.

19. The whole issue of an adequate definition of myth is still subject to much disagreement. See Henry A. Murray, ed., *Myth and Mythmaking* (Boston: Beacon Press, 1968); and Sebeok, ed., *Myth*.

Chapter 1. Masters of Life and Death

1. The most important examples of such violence involve the Vāsiṣṭha cycle, which is closely connected with several complexes of Bhārgava myth (See chapter 4).

2. *Brahmahatyā*, brahman-slaying, is generally considered the worst possible sin. See *Manu* XI.54.72 ff. See also Introduction, note 15.

3. Sukthankar, "The Bhṛgus and the Bhārata," p. 16. Muir also finds this worthy of note: "It is worthy of remark that in a legend, one object of which, at least, would seem to be to hold up to abhorrence the impiety of the Kshattriyas in oppressing the Brahmans, we should thus find a palliation of the conduct of the oppressors, coming from the other world." J. Muir, *Original Sanskrit Texts*, 5 vols. (2d ed.; Amsterdam: Oriental Press, 1967), I, 449.

4. It is not the usual practice of the epic ākhyānas to introduce such significant developments with no introduction.

5. The theme is perhaps suggested by the strange reference in the *ŚBr* according to which the Bhṛgus (or the Āñgirasas) went to heaven as a group (*ŚBr* IV.1.5.1. ff): . . . *yatra vai bhṛgavo vāñgiraso vā svargaṃ lokaṃ samāśnuvata* "At the place where the Bhṛgus or the Āñgirasas had attained the heavenly world. . . ." In the epic, Cyavana, the central figure of the *ŚBr* episode, is said to have preferred death to separation from his beloved fish (*Mbh* XIII.50–51).

A non-Bhṛguid example of brahmanical death wish may be seen in Vasiṣṭha's numerous attempts to kill himself (*Mbh* I.166.39–45).

6. The Aurvopākhyāna is emboxed in and cited as a precedent in the Vāsiṣṭha episode of Parāśara. The two stories are thematically quite simililar.

7. Cf. R 49–51.

8. Muir regards the Jamadagni-Rāma story as a "version of the Aurva episode" (*Original Sanskrit Texts*, I, 449). Sukthankar, typically, is most perceptive in suggesting, "In the above legend we may notice some of the repeated motives of Bhārgava stories. There is first of all the feud of the *kṣatriyas*, which finally *develops into the creation of the figure of the Bhārgava Rāma*, 'the foremost of all weapon-bearers,' who single-handed, with the aid of his magical weapons, the *astras*, conquers the whole earth, annihilating the Kṣatriyas thrice seven times" ("Bhṛgus and the Bhārata," p. 16; italics added). According to some Bhārgava genealogies, Jamadagni is the grandson of Aurva and the two episodes are incidents in a long-standing vendetta between the clans. See *Mbh* XIII.56.2–12 (= CK 24–34).

Many scholars have regarded the two stories as connected, and in fact as forming together a reminiscence of historical events. For a critique of such interpretations, see chapter 4.

9. See chapter 2 for further discussion of the Haihayas and their relation to the Bhṛgus.

10. Thus according to the version of the Āraṇyakaparvan, Arjuna violates Jamadagni's hospitality and steals his calf (R 44–45). On the other hand, an elaborate version in the Śāntīparvan describes him as a pious and benign prince (*Mbh* XII.49.30–33) and attributes the theft to his sons (v. 40). There is considerable evidence that the latter version is not truly Bhṛguid in the sense that the former is. I thus regard the Āraṇyaka passage as the basic epic version of the Jamadagni-Rāma myth. I have discussed this issue in some detail in "Akṛtavraṇa vs. Śrīkṛṣṇa . . . ," *ABORI* 53 (1970), 161–73.

11. Aside from his martial skills (R 24), Jamadagni is usually described as being of a wrathful and aggressive nature. See R 35–37 and *Mbh* XIII.97–98, where he is depicted as a mighty archer of the most irascible character. Cf., however, *Mbh* XIII.49.30–33, where the sage is said to be extremely tranquil. In the Aurva story the pitṛs explicitly state that they were capable of self-defense (A 30).

12. R 44–45; *Mbh* XII.49.40

13. The story is told at *Mbh* I.165 and with still greater elaboration at *Rām* I.51–56. The identity of the motif in the two contexts is obvious. See Sukthanker, "Bhṛgus and the Bhārata," pp. 23–24.

14. See *Mbh* I.93 and *HV* X.13–15.

15. Later purāṇic redactors, however, perhaps confusing the two myths or perhaps attempting to rationalize Arjuna's theft, have identified Jamadagni's cow with the kāmadhenu. Thus at *BrahmP* III.21–58, Jamadagni, like Vasiṣṭha, uses the wish-cow to show hospitality to Arjuna. In the *Reṇukā Mahātmyā*, a late

purāṇic text, Jamadagni is shown as begging the wish-cow as a boon from Indra (vv. 60–63).

16. The extensive interconnections between these two mythic cycles and between each of them and the mythology of Viśvāmitra is a phenomenon as yet little explored. It may, however, be of considerable significance to an understanding of the relation between the two Sanskrit epics.

17. It is curious that other Bhārgava myths, such as those of Aurva and Rāma, in which brahmans are slain do not make reference to the specific sin of brahmahatyā even in the denunciations of the killers. Also interesting is the fact that although Kaca technically kills Śukra in emerging from his belly, he does not appear thereby to incur this sin.

18. See chapter 3.

19. See chapter 3. It is repeated and alluded to several times in the epic (*Mbh* I.121–24; XIII.141.16–30; XV.9.31–36).

20. On the other hand, Indra is shown elsewhere as being terrified of the power of a Bhārgava boy (*Mbh* XIII.41.18). This fear is more characteristic of the god's attitude toward brahmans and their powers.

21. The death by snake-bite of Pramadvarā, the fiancée of the Bhārgava Ruru (*Mbh* I.8), should perhaps be regarded as related to this motif. It is, in any case, the nearest thing to it in the epic. The story is more pertinent as an example of another Bhṛguid motif, the resurrection of the dead.

22. The story of the beheading of Śukra's mother is the only episode considered in this study that is not to be found in the *Mbh.* It occurs in various Purāṇas, notably at *MatsyaP* 47 (ŚA), but is also found in the *BrahmaṇḍP* and at *PadmaP* I.13.202 ff. The episode is known to the *Rām.* Viśvāmitra alludes to it as precedent in his exhortation to Rāma (Dāśarathi), who is hesitant to kill a demoness: "Moreover, Rāma, Viṣṇu long ago slew Bhṛgu's wife, the mother of Kāvya, firm in her vows, who wanted to deprive the world of Indra" (*Rām.* I.24.18). Cf. pāda c, *anindraṃ lokam icchantī*, with ŚA 34, *anindrān vaḥ karomy aham.* Again, the late UK uses a concise version of the story to explain both Viṣṇu's incarnation as Rāma and the latter's separation from Sītā. The passage, found in the vulgate at VII.51.11–18, is relegated to an appendix (no. 7) by the Crit. ed.

The myth is well known to epic commentators. It is summarized by the *Bhūṣana* and *Rāmāyaṇaśiromani ṭīkās*, whose authors refer to the *MatsyaP*. Nīlakaṇṭha, the late *Mbh* commentator, gives a slightly different summary in his commentary on the *Mbh* (Citr. ed.) XII.289.7 (equals ŚŚ 7) but cites no source. I have included the *MatsyaP* episode because it illuminates the use of the motif and because I am sure that a version of the story is the source of the motif in the Āraṇyakaparvan version of the story of Reṇukā.

23. The episode has been elaborated greatly in the purāṇic literature in connection with the elevation of the protagonist to the stature of divinities and the

growth of the Paraśurāma cult. See *BrahmP* III.21–58. In South India, Reṇukā is associated with the goddess Elamma through the motif of the transposed heads. See Gustav Oppert, *The Original Inhabitants of India* (Westminster: Constable, 1873), p. 164. The episode is known also to the *Rām* (II.18.29). The story has received some scholarly attention. See especially Biardeau, "La Décapitation de Reṇukā. . . ."

Although the story of Rāma and Jamadagni is told several times in the *Mbh*, the beheading of Reṇukā appears only once in that epic and as such can hardly be regarded as an essential part of the Rāma myth there. See Goldman, "Some Observations on the Paraśu. . . ."

24. This verse marks the beginning of the answer to Yudhiṣṭhira's question at R 1. The passage from that point up until the episode of Reṇukā provides the rationale for Rāma's warlike behavior. The Reṇukā episode, aside from demonstrating Rāma's unwavering obedience, is not to the point.

25. See, for example, Kapila and the sons of Sagara at *Rām* I.37 ff. and *Mbh* III.104 ff.

26. Cf. Viśvāmitra and the Triśaṅku mvth at *Rām* I.56–59. The closest parallel to this is found in the Kauśika cycle.

27. Aside from the Bhṛgus, the only similar exception is the brahman Droṇa, epic hero and warrior-priest of the Kauravas, and even he is explicitly associated with Rāma. Sukthankar notes: "The first reference to a direct contact between a Bhārgava and one of the epic characters occurs in adhy. 121 of the Ādi. In this pseudo-historical epic, the myth may not be properly regarded as concerned with events in time. Therefore the Bhārgava Rāma who only a few chapters previously is said to have lived in the interval between the Tretā and the Dvāpara Ages is here represented as the teacher (*guru*) of Ācārya Droṇa, who lived in the interval between the Dvāpara and the Kali Ages. The pupilship is only symbolical, but the basis of the symbolism is significant. Ācārya Droṇa is the *guru* of the Kauravas and the Pāṇḍavas and of all the other valiant Kṣatriyas of the time, and he was also one of the greatest warriors on the side of the Kauravas in the Bhārata War. But Ācārya Droṇa must also have a *guru*. And who would be more suitable as *guru* than the Bhārgava Rāma, who is the foremost of all weapon-bearers (*sarvaśastrabhṛtāṃ varaḥ*)?" ("Bhṛgus and the Bhārata," p. 13). See *Mbh* I.121 and 154.

28. In some epic versions the monster begins to destroy all the other gods as well. See *Mbh* XIII.141.25; 142.2.

29. *Mbh* XIII.97.17. This episode is of particular interest in that the sage has recourse to the weapons of a warrior. See chapter 2 for a further discussion of this phenomenon.

30. *Mbh* XIII.41.20–23. The passage is interesting in that it explicitly recognizes the contradictions inherent in the notion of killing one of the immortals. Vipula warns the god: "Don't underestimate through reliance on the notion 'I am

immortal.' There is nothing that the power of asceticism cannot accomplish." *Mbh* XIII.41.26

31. This is confirmed by a reference to Aurva in another context of the *Mbh* (XIII.138.11). It is said there that Aurva destroyed the great kṣatriya race of the Tālajaṅghas by himself. The Tālajaṅghas and the Haihayas are cousins descended from Heheya and Tālajaṅgha, two kings of Śaryāti's race (*Mbh* XIII.31.7).

In some purāṇic passages Aurva is said to be the guru of Prince Sagara, to whom he gives weapons for the destruction of the Haihayas. See *VişP* IV.3.18: "When he [Sagara] had been invested with the sacred thread, Aurva taught him the Vedas, the innumerable weapons, and the Āgneyāstra, which is called the *Bhārgava*."

32. In lieu of providing any coherent explanation of Aurva's inconsistent behavior, the redactors of the passage simply repeat the sage's decision four times.

33. It is important to note in the Bhārgava context that these are all functions normally assigned to the kṣatriyas and not the brahmans.

34. Aurva's final argument (A 38,51) that the repressed anger would destroy him is also vitiated by the original purpose of that anger. This connection is traceable to the Vedas. Thus at *RV* VIII.102.4 Aurva and Bhṛgu are associated with the fire in the ocean.

35. For a discussion of the vedic antecedents of the myth of Aurva and the horse-head fire, see Wendy D. O'Flaherty's "The Submarine Mare in the Mythology of Śiva," *JRAS*, no. 1 (1971), p. 22.

36. *Mbh* I.69.9 ff.

37. *Mbh* I.169.7.

38. *Mbh* I.172.2–3. The motif of a genocidal sacrifice is important in the genesis of the whole *Mahābhārata* story: the epic is recited at Janamejaya's great snake sacrifice, which he institutes to avenge his father. Curiously enough, a Bhārgava parallel is also cited there in order to make the king desist. This is the story of Ruru's genocidal vendetta against the snakes (*Mbh* I.13–53 and I.8–12).

39. *Mbh* I.172.14–17. The motif is unquestionably a version of the horse-head fire motif of the Aurva story and is undoubtedly its source. The sacrificial fire of Parāśara has become the metaphoric fire of Aurva's wrath, which in turn becomes the Vāḍavānala. Several other minor motifs, such as that of the sole surviving embryo and the critical effect of the mother's intervention, have evidently been borrowed as well.

40. This is similar to the explanation offered by Aurva's murdered ancestors, that they were quite happy to be killed.

41. Sukthankar notes: "the Bhārgava most popular with our bards is surely Rāma Jāmadagnya. The bards love to dwell on his martial exploits, repeating them whenever the slightest opportunity for it presents itself. The shadow of this colossus overspreads the entire epic, excepting the short tail at the

end of the poem. In our epic he is not yet a full-fledged avatar, but on the high way to be elevated to that rank, surreptitious efforts being made to make the epic document his divinity. He conquers the whole world, alone and unaided; such is the prowess of his fierce austerities. He frees the earth of the burden of the Kṣatriyas thrice seven times and makes the gift of the earth to Kaśyapa, his priest, who divides it among the Brahmins. Rāma fights even the enemies of the gods, with the same assurance and success, enemies whom the gods themselves could not subdue. As the Bhārgava Rāma is the perfect warrior (sarvaśastrabhṛtāṃ varaḥ, a phrase the bards love to apply to him), three of the leading warriors of the Kaurava army—Bhīṣma, Droṇa, and Karṇa—are said to have been initiated into the science of arms by Rāma Jāmadagnya, though the latter according to the epic itself, lived at the end of the Tretā Age and the Kuru-Pāṇḍava war took place at the end of the Dvāpara" ("Bhṛgus and the Bhārata," p. 18).

42. See above, note 22, for a discussion of the possible source of this motif.

43. Elsewhere in the epic Rāma is said to have fought and killed the demon enemies of the gods (*Mbh* VIII.24.144), fought a duel with the hero Bhīṣma (*Mbh* V.185.17) and even to have challenged the kṣatriya hero Rāma Dāśarathi (*Mbh* Citr. ed., III.99.34 ff.; *Rām* I.73–75). The last two of these exploits, although in keeping with Rāma's role as the scourge of the warrior class, differ from the central Rāma myth in that they are contemporary with the events of the epic stories of the *Mbh* and *Rām*, respectively, and because from neither one does a Bhārgava emerge victorious. These episodes have, therefore, little bearing on the true Bhārgava corpus.

44. There are numerous versions and allusions to the career of Bhārgava Rāma in the *Mbh*. See *Mbh* I.58, 98, III.115–17 (=R), XII.49, XIII.4.55–56. See also Appendix I, no. 8, lines 828–72 of the Droṇaparvan in the Crit. ed. In all, Sukthankar counted some ten variants of the line, *triḥsaptakṛtvaḥ pṛthivīṃ kṛtvā niḥkṣatriyāṃ prabhuḥ* ("That lord, having rendered the earth free from kṣatriyas twenty-one times"), while reference to the event is made some twenty times. Sukthankar, "Bhṛgus and the Bhārata," p. 65.

45. See chapter 4.

46. Another obvious but less significant connection may be the fact that in the Śāntiparvan account of Rāma's career, the Aurvopākhyāna motif of slaughter of the unborn children appears again. There it is the kṣatriyas who are the victims. Cf. A 8 and 42 with *Mbh* XII.49.55.

47. I would consider the motif of the restoration of youth to be a variant. It plays a crucial role in the myths of Cyavana and the Aśvins and of the Bhārgava sage Uttaṅka (*Mbh* XIV.55.21–24). It is also central to the famous story of Yayāti (*Mbh* I.73–80). The motif in the latter story, which has many Bhārgava connections, is closely bound up with the figure of Śukra, who is elsewhere the special custodian of the life-restorative magic. Cf. *RV* I.117, *Mbh* I.73–80. See

also E. Washburn Hopkins, "The Fountain of Youth," *JAOS* 26, pt. 1 (1905), 1–67, and S.A. Dange, "Virgin and the Divine Seed Layer (*RgV* X.61)," *JIH* 24, pt. 2 (1967), 369–98.

48. The motif occurs with some frequency in the epic, purāṇic, and nītī literature. Nowhere, however, is it associated with one particular group so regularly as it is with the Bhṛgus. For references to the motif in the literature, see *Mbh* XIII.12.43 and XIII.5.28.

Readers may also be familiar with the many examples from the *Kathāsaritsāgara Pañcatantra*, *Vetālapañcaviṃśati*, etc. For further examples see the entries "Restored to life . . .", "Restoring dead to life," "Resuscitation of Angamanjari . . ." and "Resuscitation" in the index to C. H. Tawney, tr., *The Ocean of Story* (Somadeva's *Kathāsaritsāgara*), ed. by N. M. Penzer, 10 vols. (London: Sawyer, 1924), vol. 10. The exceptions are Jamadagni and the Bhṛgus of the Aurvopākhyāna.

49. Bhṛgu, Jamadagni, Ruru, and Śukra.

50. The terseness of the account, similar to that of the account of Arjuna's theft of Jamadagni's cow, perhaps suggests hasty inclusion of the motif.

51. *Mbh* I.8–12. This episode marks the conclusion of an important Bhārgava passage that, as Sukthankar observed ("Bhṛgus and the Bhārata," pp. 60–62, 65, and 67–68), constitutes a new Bhṛguid beginning to the epic. The story has attained some popularity with storytellers, recurring in one form or another in the *Kathāsaritsāgara* and the *Pañcatantra*.

52. *Mbh* I.8.14–18.

53. *Mbh* I.9.4–5. Ruru's reference to brahmanical conduct (*brāhmaṇadharma*) is similar to Bhṛgu's at ŚA 49.

54. *Mbh* I.9.6.

55. *Mbh* I.9.8.

56. *Mbh* I.9.10.

57. *Mbh* I.9.13–16. Cf. ŚA 51. Ruru's bargain is reminiscent of Puru's well-known exchange of his youth for Yayāti's senility in the Yayātyupākhyāna of the *Mbh*.

58. The terms *mṛtasaṃjīvinī*, *saṃjīvinī*, etc., are, elsewhere in the literature, applied to various magical objects, jewels, plants, etc. The spell itself is mentioned in other contexts. For references to the various magical articles and spells, see Tawney, *Ocean of Story*, I.25–29, "Notes on the 'Magical Articles' Motif in Folklore"; and Hopkins, "Fountain of Youth."

59. This is not the case, however, in all the Purāṇas. See, for example, *Brahmāṇḍ P* III.30.42 ff., where Bhṛgu uses the spell to revive Jamadagni.

60. *PadmaP* VI.146; *Mbh* I.73–80.

61. ŚK 7–9 specifically states that Bṛhaspati was ignorant of the vidyā and through its use the asuras were defeating the gods. Śukra is well known as a

disciple of Śiva. Their relationship is made explicit at *PadmaP* VI.146.1–5: "Śrīmahādeva said: I will tell you of another (*tīrtha*,) the excellent Durdharṣeśvara, by the mere memory of which even a sinful man becomes full of merit. The place at which Uśanas, scion of the Bhārgavas, fulfilled a terrible (*durdharṣa*) vow, when the war of gods and the demons was over and the daityas had been killed, and at which, having propitiated the terrible (*durdharṣa*) Mahādeva, cause of the worlds (*lokakāraṇam*), he received, for the sake of the daityas, a spell for the revival of the dead (*mṛtasañjīvinī vidyā*) from Tryambaka [Śiva], is renowned as a *tīrtha* throughout the world. A person who bathes at the Kāvyatīrtha, having worshiped Mahādeva under the name of Durdharṣeśvara, is freed from all sins."

The use of the epithet *tryambaka* in verse 3 in connection with his boon of the saṃjīvinī vidyā is probably not accidental. The verse—*tryambakaṃ yajāmahe*, etc.—that occurs at *RV* VII.59.12 and is repeated widely in the vedic literature (see M. Bloomfield, *A Vedic Concordance* [Cambridge, Mass: Harvard University, 1906]) is often considered, because of its plea—*mṛtyor mukṣīya māmṛtāt*—to be the saṃjīvinī mantra par excellence. The verse is also repeated in some MSS. of the *Mbh*. For the citations, see the critical apparatus to the Śāntiparvan, Appendix I, no. 8, line 183 (Crit. ed., vol. 16, p. 2059).

62. Yet such is the attraction of the motif for the mythmakers that it begins to appear, in spite of its uselessness, in some purāṇic versions of the story of the Bhārgava Rāma. For example, at *BrahmāṇḍP* III.30.42 ff., Bhṛgu himself appears and revives Jamadagni using the saṃjīvinī vidyā. Here, however, so that the essential theme of genocidal revenge can be retained, Jamadagni is killed again, this time for good.

63. This motif is evidently connected with a rite of initiation. It is similar in many respects to the initiation myths recorded in several areas, and in its more elaborate epic form, the Śukra-Kaca episode, explicitly involves a brahmanical initiation. See S. A. Dange, "Death and Rebirth in Initiation Ceremonies," *Indian Antiquary* 1 (3d. ser., 1964), 104–9, and M. Eliade, *Rites and Symbols of Initiation* (New York: Harper & Row, 1963), pp. 7–17.

64. *Mbh* I.72.13–14. It is curious that Kaca regards Devayānī as having dwelt in her father's "belly," perhaps in the form of semen. The situation is reminiscent of the encounter between Yama and Yamī at *RV* X.10. See R. P. Goldman, "Mortal Man and Immortal Woman: a New Interpretation of Three Ākhyāna Hymns of the Ṛgveda," *JOIB* 18, no. 4 (1969) 273–303.

65. This may be in addition to the wealth he steals from Kubera.

Chapter 2. Masters of the Earth

1. A major statement on the question of the relative status of the two varṇas is made at *Mbh* XIII.137–42, the Pavanārjunasaṃvāda, in which the

kṣatriya case is argued by the old enemy of the Bhṛgus, Arjuna Kārtavīrya, only to be refuted by Pavana, the Wind God, who cites twelve myths illustrative of brahmanical superiority. For a discussion of this critical issue in ancient India, see E. W. Hopkins, *The Mutual Relations of the Four Castes According to the Mānavadharmaśāstra* (Leipzig: Breitkopf and Hartel, 1881). A similar study for the Brāhmaṇa and Sūtra literature has been done by Albrecht F. Weber in "Collectanea über die Kaster verhältnisse in den Brāhmaṇa und Sūtra," in Weber, ed., *Indische Studien* (Berlin: F. Dummler, 1850–63; and Leipzig: A. Brockhaus, 1865–98), vol. X. The most comprehensive and valuable treatment of the subject from the standpoint of the present study is provided by John Muir in vol. I of *Original Sanskrit Texts* (2d ed.; Amsterdam: Oriental Press, 1967), which is subtitled "Mythical and Legendary Accounts of the Origin of Caste, with an Enquiry into its Existence in the Vedic Age."

2. See Introduction, note 6.

3. The theme of the tension between the two varṇas is so pervasive in the cycle that it appears even in connections that do not basically involve human kṣatriyas at all. Compare the argument between Devayānī and Sarmiṣṭhā, the daughters respectively of Śukra and the asura king Vṛṣaparvan, at *Mbh* I.73.8–11 ff.

4. In the genealogy of the Bhṛgus given at *Mbh* I.60 the line of descent of the Bhārgava Rāma runs Cyavana, Aurva, Ṛcīka, Jamadagni, and Rāma. A similar list is given by Cyavana at *Mbh* XIII.56, but, though he implies his direct ancestry of the line of Aurva, he does not explicitly state it. Thus, the Aurvopākhyāna is either unaware of this tradition or, more likely, suppresses it. To state it in the context of the Aurvopākhyāna would be to put Cyavana among those murdered by the sons of Kṛtavīrya. This would be the only record of such an event in the epic and would, in fact, run counter to the tradition according to which Cyavana, along with Śukra and Rāma, is a great, fearsome, and unconquerable being (see chapter 4).

The most important non-Bhārgava myths involving this theme are those which grow out of the famous rivalry between Vasiṣṭha and Viśvāmitra. The story has vedic antecedents and is elaborated with much subsidiary material in both epics (see *Mbh* I.165–72 and IX.41 and *Rām* I.51–56). There is a good deal of evidence that the myths of Vasiṣṭha and Viśvāmitra have influenced the myths of the Aurva-Rāma subcycle considerably. The vedic references to the two sages as well as the epic accounts of their rivalry and the elevation of Viśvāmitra to the rank of brahman have been the subject of much scholarly attention. The former are treated at length by Roth in vol. 3 of *Zur Literature und Geschichte des Veda* (Stuttgart: A. Leisching, 1846), and also by Muir, *Original Sanskrit Texts*, pp. 317–34 (Vasiṣṭha) and 337–49 (Viśvāmitra). Muir has also provided the texts and translations of the principal epic passages concerning the rivalry of the two sages and the change of Viśvāmitra's status (pp. 388–426). Christian Lassen also offered some interpretive remarks on the subject of the legends of the rivalry between Vasiṣṭha and Viśvāmitra on what must be described as historical lines; see *Indische Alterthumskunde* (Leipzig: L. A. Kittler, 1867), vol. I, pp. 718 ff.

5. Several modern scholars have regarded Rāma's slaughter of the kṣatriyas as the culmination of a family feud. See chapter 4 for a discussion of this interpretation.

6. The idea is suggested by an interesting passage (*Mbh* XIII.56) that will be discussed at length below.

7. The story is the oldest attested Bhārgava myth with epic currency. Cf. *ŚBr* IV.1.1 ff. and *JBr* III.121.

8. *Mbh* XIII.52. This lengthy section is omitted from the CK translation.

9. *Mbh* XIII.52.8–9, 13.

10. *Mbh* I.169.11.

11. *Mbh* XIII.31.5–7.

12. *Mbh* XIII.34.42–54.

13. Cyavana is said to sacrifice for Śaryāta in various passages of the Brāhmaṇa literature (e.g., *JBr* III.128). His hostile encounter with the Śāryātas is also well known to these texts (*ŚB* IV.1.5 ff.).

The *AV* seems to know of hostility between the Bhṛgus and the Vaitahavyas. There a group called the Sṛñjaya Vaitahavyas are said to have suffered for having injured the Bhṛgus (*AV* V.19.1). This may well refer to a legend which became the prototype for the epic myths of Bhārgava-Haihaya hostility.

14. This does not apply to the episodes in the epic in which Rāma is said to be the contemporary and guru of several of the heroes of the Bhārata war (see Sukthankar, "Bhṛgus and the Bhārata," p. 13). However, though these episodes are of great significance to the question of the Bhṛguid recension of the *Mbh*, they do not bear significantly on the issue of the Bhṛguid-kṣatriya relations in the Bhārgava cycle itself.

The theme of Rāma as a guru of the kṣatriyas is paralleled by the popular purāṇic account of Aurva's teaching of the dhanurveda to the Prince Sagara, so that the latter could destroy the Haihayas and Tālajañghas who had slain his father. See *VisP* IV.3.18; *Liñgapurāṇa* I.66; *Nāradapurāṇa* I.8; *MatsyaP* 12; *BhP* IX.8.23. The story is evidently a thematic variant of the Rāma story.

15. This liaison is known to the vedic version of the Cyavana myth (see *RV* I.117.6, *ŚBr* IV.1.5.1 ff, *JBr* 3.121).

16. *Mbh* I.60.44–45

17. The phrase *manoḥ kanyā*, "Manu's daughter," in the sense of any female descendant of Manu, would apply to Sukanyā. Moreover, it is possible that the term *sukanyā*, "excellent maiden," traceable to *RV* I.117.6, was not originally a proper noun but has been simply used as such in C.

18. *Mbh* I.60.45.

19. The episode is repeated and elaborated elsewhere. Cf. *BhP* 9.15.5–11; *Mbh* XIII.4.7–10, 29, XIII.56.1; *ViṣP* 4.7; *Mbh* XII.49.

20. *Mbh* XII.49.27; XIII (= CK 23). R and the later Anuś version (XIII.56) do not name Satyavatī. The name is given in the Śānti and earlier Anuś versions.

21. There is some uncertainty about Prasenajit's affiliation. Sukthankar in "The Bhṛgus and the Bhārata" (p. 63) identifies him as the king of Ayodhyā, and so, a descendant of the Ikṣvāku line. Citrav Śāstrī understands there to be two kings of this name; See S. S. Chitrav, *Bhāratavarṣīya Prācīna Caritrakośa* (Poona: Bharatiya Caritrakośa Mandal, 1964), p. 478. The vulgate text of the Harivaṃśa identifies Reṇukā's father as the Ikṣvāku monarch Reṇu. HV (Citr. ed.) I.27.38–39 = Crit. ed. app. 6B line 83.

22. *Manu* I. 10. "These six are known in the Smṛtis [lit. "are remembered"] as degraded (*apasada*); the sons of a brahman by women of the three [lower] varṇas; the sons of a king by a woman of the two [lower] varṇas; and the sons of a vaiśya by a woman of the one [lower] varṇa." The term appears in at least one Bhārgava context in a pejorative sense. Thus in the Śānti version of Rāma's career, Satyavatī begs of Ṛcīka that her son not be a *brāhmaṇāpasada*, a brahman with kṣatriya inclinations.

23. Except for Satyavatī's plea, this issue is not explicitly mentioned in the various Bhārgava myths. It is not, however, wholly overlooked, and a desire to avoid this varṇasaṃkara is the motivating force behind Cyavana's plan to destroy the Kauśika race in the Cyavanakuśikasaṃvāda of *Mbh* XIII.52–56 (= CK). See chapter 4 for a discussion of the possible implications of this mixing of the varṇas.

24. *Mbh* I.5.11 ff.

25. The name is associated with the daughters of various asuras in the purāṇic literature. See *ViṣP* I.21, where Pulomā (a wife of Kaśyapa) is said to have been the daughter of the daitya Vaiśvānara and the mother of the cruel dānavas known as Paulomas. Also suggestive is the fact that in the story she had been chosen first by the rākṣasa Puloman (*Mbh* I.5.19 ff.). Purāṇic sources identify Divyā, daughter of the asura Hiraṇyakaśipu and mother of Śukra, as another wife of Bhṛgu (*MatsyaP* 247.9; *BrahmaP* 73.31–34). The sage also had a kṣatriya wife Ūrjavatī (*BhP* V.1.24). Still other sources name Khyāti as Bhṛgu's wife, while Śukra's mother is called Uṣā (e.g., *Viṣṇudharmottarapurāṇa* I.106).

26. At *Mbh* V.115.3 Śataparvā is named as his wife.

27. *Mbh* I.8.5.

28. *Mbh* I.8.2, XIII.31.6.

29. Sukthankar, "Bhṛgus and the Bhārata," p. 63. Pratiloma marriages are those in which the wife is of a higher social class than that of her husband. This

is considered an inversion of the correct practice and as such is not normally acceptable. The sons of such a marriage are said to be *sūtas*, or bards, considered a degraded class. See *Manu* X.11.

30. The practice of military occupation by brahmans is a violation of the *varṇāśramadharma*, the social order whereby each class has its own proper duties. The classic statement on this is made at *BhG* 3.35: "Better is one's own duty (*dharma*) imperfect than another's duty well done. Better is death in one's own duty; another's duty brings danger."

Moreover, the *Mbh* specifically lists soldiering along with entertainment as disqualifying brahmans from participating in the sacrifice: "Singers, actors, tumblers, musicians, storytellers and warriors, O king, are not worthy of an invitation [to the sacrifice]" (*Mbh* XIII.24.16). Of great interest in this context is a passage (*Mbh* XIII.29) in which Indra, in his efforts to dissuade the low-born Mataṅga from his attempts to attain brahmanhood, lists the various births through which one who is destined for this exalted position must first pass. The god declares that there is a hierarchy within the rank of brahmanhood as well as in human society generally. Brahmans who live by the sword are stated to be but one level above the despised *brahmabandhus*, brahmans by birth only, and some distance below truly learned brahmans and even those who know only the gāyatrī. These warrior brahmans are said to be characterized by *kāṇḍapṛṣthatā* (*Mbh* XIII.29.10–11). This term is explained by Nīl. as meaning the state of living by arms. The term *kāṇḍapṛṣtha* is also used pejoratively of anyone who turns his back on his hereditary career, caste, etc. It is interesting to note that in Bhavabhūti's famous drama the *Mahāvīracarita* (Act 3, v. 3, Nirnaya Sagara ed.), the brahman Śatānanda uses this term to describe the Bhārgava Rāma. In the light of these two passages, the failure to apply the term to Rāma in the *Mahābhārata* takes on considerable significance.

31. See note 14 to chapter 2 for references in the literature. The Bhārgavas' association with the dhanurveda is so close for the purāṇic bards that one of the divine weapons, the Āgneyāstra, is also called the Bhārgavāstra. See ViṣP IV.3.18 quoted above in note 31 to chapter 1. This too harks back to the vedic association of the Bhṛgus and fire (*agni*).

32. *Mbh* XIII.97–98.

33. *Mbh* XII.49.27.

34. *Mbh* XII.49.29. Elsewhere in the *Mbh* Rāma is said to have received his weapons and the skill to use them from Śiva (*Mbh* VIII.24.154–55).

35. See Goldman, "Aṛktavraṇa vs. Śrīkṛṣṇa."

36. See also *Mbh* XII.49.56 ff.

37. The circumstances surrounding Rāma's abandonment of the earth and restoration of the kṣatriyas vary considerably in the various versions of the myth. Compare, for example, R 64–68 and *Mbh* XII.49.56–57.

38. R 16–22 (= *Mbh* III.115.22–30), *Mbh* XII.49.1–34, *Mbh* XIII.4.21–46, *Mbh* XIII.13.52–56 (= CK).

39. R 16–22 (= *Mbh* III.115.22–30) and *Mbh* XII.49.1–34.

40. CK 9 (= *Mbh* XII.52 ff.).

41. *Mbh* XIII.4.

42. The most important of these are the stories centering around the conflict of Vasiṣṭha and Viśvāmitra (*Mbh* I.165, IX.39, and *Rām* I.51–56). At *Mbh* V. 104.17–18 Viśvāmitra, after a prolonged course of austerities, is acknowledged as a brahman by Dharma.

43. Such a metamorphosis is exceedingly rare in the literature. At *ŚBr* XI.6.2.10 the famous king Janaka is said to have become a brahman. The only other such change in the epic besides Viśvāmitra's occurs, significantly enough, in another Bhṛguid context. This is the story of Vītahavya, *Mbh* XIII.31. Elsewhere in the epic (*Mbh* XIII.28–30) Indra categorically denies the possibility of elevation to brahmanhood in a single lifetime for one of low birth or whose mind is not purified (*akṛtātman*); *Mbh* XIII.28.26–28.

44. *Mbh* XII.49.21; cf. R 21. See also CK 6,32–36, where an attempt to restore symmetry is made. Although all principal versions of Rāma's origin agree on the point of the skipped generation, they differ sharply in their description of Satyavatī's son, Jamadagni. The version of the Śāntiparvan represents the warlike proclivities as having passed over Jamadagni, who is described as tranquil and devoted to penances (*Mbh* XIII.49.27). The martial characteristics do not appear until the birth of Rāma. The Āraṇyakaparvan version, on the other hand, shows Jamadagni as being a master of the dhanurveda (R 24), despite the alteration of the boon. Rāma, moreover, is not described as being especially interested in warfare until after his murder of Reṇukā, when he requests invulnerability in battle (R 42). Later on in the version, however, Jamadagni is shown as passive and helpless, while his son is violent and aggressive (R 50,59–62).

These differences in characterization have to do with both internal issues in the Bhārgava corpus and also the general context of the two versions. See also Goldman, "Akṛtavraṇa vs. Śrīkṛṣṇa."

45. It is perhaps of significance that the sages Viśvāmitra and Jamadagni are associated in one or two passages in the veda. There the sages are said to have together gained cattle. See *PBr* XIII.5.15 and *JBr* III.238. Cf. also *RV* X.167.4.

46. *Mbh* XIII.52.1–6.

47. *Mbh* XIII.52.10. Because of the length and repetitiveness of the Cyavanakuśikasaṃvāda, only portions of it are translated as the myth of Cyavana and Kuśika (CK). These are *Mbh* XIII.52.1–9 (CK 1–9), XIII.55.9–12, 27b–35 (CK 10–22), and the whole of XIII.56 (CK 23–42).

48. *Mbh* XIII.55.2–8.

49. See CK note 2.

50. But see CK note 4.

51. The first thing that must strike a reader of the Cyavanakuśikasaṃvāda is the great length that the episode requires to present, after all, very little in the way of narrative development. In the first place, the various provocations that Cyavana inflicts upon the king and his wife, although they really all amount to the same thing, are each related at some length so that, with the description of the wonderful palace, the account occupies the bulk of the three adhyāyas 52–54, a total of some 125 verses. And, as if this were not enough, Kuśika, in asking the propitiated sage for the explanation of his curious behavior, is made to occupy an additional seven ślokas in recapitulating each of the sage's actions in his question (XIII.55.2–8). Yet even this is not the end of this recapitulation. Cyavana in explaining his actions feels it necessary to comment upon how dangerous it would have been for the king or his wife to have shown anger or jealousy in each instance of his provocative behavior. Thus he requires some 13 additional ślokas to repeat the same material for yet a third time (55.14–26) and still 3 more to repeat Kuśika's remarks of the previous adhyāya on the relative value of brahmanhood and kingship (55.27–29).

52. The question of the "third man" has led the author or authors of the passage to some apparent confusion regarding the Bhārgava family history as recorded in the other versions. Thus it appears that Jamadagni, and not his father Ṛcīka, is to marry Gādhi's daughter (CK 31–34). It is also likely that Cyavana stresses the revelation of the dhanurveda, the unequivocal testament to the Bhārgavas' role inversion, to Ṛcīka, for the same reason. According to this reckoning, Rāma, the only real practitioner of the martial arts among the Bhṛgus, represents the third generation of martial Bhārgavas. It is possible that the idea was to align more closely the generations of Rāma and Viśvamitra. In the other versions, the latter is the great-uncle of the former. Here he would be his uncle.

53. Of this formula, Sukthankar notes: "It occurs, with slight variations, over and over again in our Mahābhārata, its exultant note ringing like a distant echo in the remotest corners and crevices of this huge epos, which was composed by Kṛṣṇa Dvaipāyana to spread in this world the fame of the high-souled Pāṇḍavas and of other puissant *Kṣatriyas*" ("The Bhṛgus and the Bhārata," p. 7).

54. Viśvāmitra is mentioned here as the only other example of such a change. His story, however, is not related. See Muir, *Original Sanskrit Texts*, I, 440–42.

55. These, the Haihayas and their cousins the Tālajaṅghas, are, of course, the traditional patrons and hereditary foes of the Bhṛgus. See also note 13 above. The Śāryātas are the patrons and kinsmen of Cyavana.

56. *Mbh* XIII.31.11–23.

57. Ibid., vv. 23–26. It is most interesting to note here that Divodāsa claims (vv. 24–25) that his race has been exterminated by the wicked Vaitahavyas. Thus like Cyavana in the *ŚBr* and Aurva in the epic he exemplifies the motif of the sole survivor.

58. Ibid., vv. 28–29.

59. Ibid., vv. 29–40.

60. Ibid., v. 42.

61. Ibid., vv. 44–47.

62. Ibid., v. 48.

63. Ibid., v. 49.

64. The Udyogaparvan version of Viśvāmitra's elevation is similarly accomplished by the mere word of Dharma (*Mbh* V.104.17–18).

65. *Mbh* XIII.31.51–52.

66. Ibid., vv. 54 ff. Ruru and Pramati are known from the Ruru episode of the *Mbh* as the grandson and son, respectively, of Cyavana (*Mbh* I.8.1–2). It is the former who gives half his life for his bride. Śaunaka, the sage under whose auspices the great sacrifice is undertaken that is the occasion for the recitation of the *Mahābhārata*, is another relatively important descendant of this Bhārgava branch. He is evidently the son of Ruru's son Śunaka (ibid.). It is especially interesting to note here that these descendants of Vītahavya, who is a Śāryāta by birth and a Bhṛgu by nomination, are also said in this Ādiparvan genealogy to be the immediate descendants of the Bhārgava Cyavana and the Śāryāta princess Sukanyā. This is a suggestive bit of overdetermination.

67. Cf. *Mbh* XIII.31.40. and R 48.

Chapter 3. The Masters of Heaven

1. Even where supernatural intervention occurs it is not the gods, but the Bhārgava pitṛs who usually assume the role of the *dei ex machina*. See A 28, R 63.

2. Some of the motifs whereby the hostility is expressed may be borrowed from or influenced by the myths of other sages. These myths, however, usually belong to cycles having special affiliation with the Bhārgava cycle, especially those involving sages of the Vāsiṣṭha, Kauśika, or Āṅgirasa class.

Thus, compare Indra's encounter with the Kauśika Viśvāmitra (*Rām* I.56–59) and the Āṅgirasa Saṃvarta (*Mbh* XIV.9) with the same motif in the Cyavana myth (C 69–70). Cf. also the paralysis of Indra by Bhṛgu's wife at ŚA 35.

3. Sukthankar, "Bhṛgus and the Bhārata," p. 21.

4. *Mbh* XIV. 52.20

5. *Mbh* XIV.53.5, 54.1.

6. Confirmation of this idea may be found in the fact that, although Uttañka plays an important role in instigating the famous snake sacrifice of Janamejaya (*Mbh* I.3.73 ff.), he is not there identified as a Bhṛgu. See Sukthankar, "Bhṛgus and the Bhārata," pp. 57–59.

7. One of these myths, however, may be cited as an example of the way in which sectarian traditions may build upon a preexisting Bhṛguid tradition. According to a popular Vaiṣṇava tradition represented by various versions in various purāṇic texts (See *BhP* X.89; *PadmaP* [ASS] VI. 282), Bhṛgu is deputed by the great seers to test the virtues of each of the three great divinities, Śiva, Brahman, and Viṣṇu, and to report back to them as to which of the gods is most worthy of worship. According to various versions, Bhṛgu insults or is insulted by Śiva and Brahman. In the *PadmaP* version he even curses Śiva. The two gods are, however, either unwilling or unable to retaliate against the sage. Finally, Bhṛgu, finding Viṣṇu asleep, actually kicks the god. Viṣṇu responds to the outrage with humility and is accordingly declared the greatest of the gods. The thrust of this myth is sectarian: the exaltation of Viṣṇu among the gods. However, it seems to me to be more than likely that Bhṛgu, of all the great sages, is chosen for this terrifying task because of the well-established epic tradition of the sage and his descendants as men used to dealing on terms of equality with the gods—as men who do not fear the gods but whom, rather, the gods have every reason to fear.

8. *PadmaP* 47 (=ŚA), V.13.202 ff.

9. The rationale of the curse is that since Viṣṇu has violated dharma in slaying a woman, he must take human form to protect dharma. In another version, Bhṛgu curses Viṣṇu to have 10 avatars for failing to guard the sage's sacrifice from the asuras (*PadmaP* II.121).

10. *Mbh.* XII.278 (=ŚŚ) Also, in a famous Vaiṣṇava myth of the Purāṇas, Bhṛgu is cast in the role of the arbiter of the great gods. In pursuance of this commission he insults Śiva and his own father, Brahman. See *BhP* X.89.

11. Cyavana's association with the Aśvins is established in the *RV* (*RV* I.116.10, I.117.13, I.118.6, V.74.5, VI.62.7, VII.68.6, VII.71.5, X.39.4, X.59.1). The *ŚBr* (and *JBr*) accounts of his rejuvenation state that he rewards them by giving them information that leads to their inclusion in the soma sacrifice (*ŚBr* IV.1.5.10 ff, *JBr* III.121). The relevant antecedent for the epic version, however, is to be found at *JBr* III.159–61, where Indra objects to Cyavana's making an offering of a *graha*, a sacrificial ladle, to the Asvins. Vidanvat, another Bhārgava sage, then objects to Indra's own ladle. A violent altercation arises between the gods and the ṛsis which ends only when the latter create the asura Mada and the gods realize the superiority of the sages.

12. See *Mbh* XII.141.16–30; XIV.9.31–36. The story has wide currency in postepic literature as well. See Hopkins, "Fountain of Youth," pp. 50 off.

13. *Mbh* XIII.40–43.

14. *Mbh* XIII.41.18.

15. *Mbh* XIII.41.20–23. The reference in v. 21 is to Indra's similar encounter with Ahalyā and her husband Gautama. The episode is extremely well known. Cf. *Rām* VII.30 off; *Mbh* XIII.41; *KSS* XVII.21 (Tawney, tr., *Ocean of Story*, II, 45–46).

16. *Mbh* XIII.41.25–27.

17. The implication of the section (*Mbh* I.5–12) has been discussed by Sukthankar; see "Bhṛgus and the Bhārata," pp. 60–62.

18. *Mbh* I.5.17–18.

19. *Mbh* I.5.26.

20. *Mbh* I.6.1–3. The motif of the effulgent birth is also associated with Aurva, Cyavana's son. It is probable that the Aurvopākhyāna has borrowed the motif from the Paulomaparvan. See also note 39, chapter 1.

21. *Mbh* I.6.10.

22. *Mbh* I.6.13. The curse derives its power from the brahmanical obsession with questions of purity and impurity.

23. *Mbh* I.7.21.

24. *Mbh* XIII.97.9–11.

25. *Mbh* XIII.97.17.

26. *Mbh* XIII.98.2–7.

27. *Mbh* XIII.98.10–22.

28. One might, however, include the Anuś version of the Nahuṣa-Agastya myth in which Bhṛgu, on behalf of Agastya, curses Nahuṣa, who had become the king of the gods, to fall from his lofty state. See Sukthankar, "Bhṛgus and the Bhārata," pp. 54–56, where the Anuś version is cited as a prime example of "Bhṛguization." Compare *Mbh* V.11–17 and *Mbh* XIII.102–3.

29. *Mbh* XII.141.25. In the following adhyāya the near-swallowing of the gods is mentioned again. There it is also stated that "When the gods, along with Indra, were in Mada's mouth, Cyavana took the earth from them" (*Mbh* XIII.142.2). This idea is reminiscent of and may be related to Rāma's taking the earth from the slaughtered kṣatriyas.

30. Such explanations are, of course, common in myth, and the Bhārgava-kṣatriya episodes are not wholly free of them. Thus, the Aurva story is used to account for the great undersea horse-headed fire. Such passages are, however, sporadic and are rarely of such interest as in the tales of the Bhṛgus and the gods.

31. Some scholars restrict the term "myth" to stories that provide such explanations. See M. Eliade, *Myth and Reality* (New York: Harper and Row, 1963), pp. 21–38.

32. C 79, etc. An interesting problem about this episode, and its antecedents in the Brāhmaṇas, concerns the exclusion of the Aśvins in the first place. The

RV seems to regard them as gods worthy of praise and sacrifices. Evidently, however, there was a tradition that these figures were brought into the brahmanical pantheon at a relatively late date. The role of the Bhṛgus as their advocates against the objections of the established divinities is most provocative. See chapter 4 for further discussion of this point.

33. See note 8, chapter 3.

34. This question, although it is formally answered at v. 32, remains obscure. Nīl's explanation is that Śukra, like Vasiṣṭha and others of the seven sages, has both a terrestial and a heavenly form, but that unlike them he is unable in his earthly guise to move through the sky. I am not aware of any other references to Śukra that bear on this issue. Interestingly, however, Nīl. in his commentary on v. 32 remarks that: "His [Śukra's] heavenly motion was blocked just like that of Rāma Jāmadagnya." This latter reference is evidently to the well known passage in the *Rāmāyaṇa* in which Rāma Dāśarathi destroys the [heavenly] worlds which had been won by Rāma Jāmadagnya, although he does not destroy what appears to be the Bhārgava's ability to move through the air. See *Rām* I.75.15–16. The second question, about the enmity of the gods and asuras, goes unanswered in this passage. There are at least two purāṇic references to the legend of Śukra swallowed by Śiva. At *PadmaP* V. 13.303 Śukra alludes to his being swallowed by the god, while at *VāmanaP* 43.25–44. Śiva, while fighting the demon Andhaka, swallows Śukra to prevent him from using the saṃjīvanī spell! For this latter reference I am indebted to Dr. Wendy O'Flaherty.

35. Nīl. in his commentary on the passage offers the following ingenious if obscure explanation. Since the śūla was bent by hand (*pāṇinā anāmayat*), it came to be called *pināka* by a conjunction of the first and last sounds of the first word (*p* and *i* from *pāṇi*), the middle two of the second word (*n* and *ā* from *anāmayat*) and the nominalizing suffix *ka*. This is, at any rate, the way in which I read the commentary. It is not without problems. Belvalkar's critical notes to the passage in the Crit. ed. offer another interpretation of Nīl.'s argument based on the word *pāṇinā* alone (vol. 16, pp. 2204–05). In either case the etymology is fantastic, although something of the sort is surely implied in what otherwise is an obscure non sequitur.

36. *Mbh* XIII.41.20.

37. Actually the various vedic texts identify Bhṛgu as either the son of Brahman (Prajāpati) or of Varuṇa. According to Sukthankar, the *Mbh*, in one version of the birth of Bhṛgu, attempts to synthesize the two traditions. "Bhṛgus and the Bhārata," pp. 9–10.

38. The relationship plays a part in a number of purāṇic myths. Most notable of these is the famous episode in which Bhṛgu tests the gods Brahman, Śiva, and Viṣṇu by insulting them in turn. Thus, in the *BhP* version Brahman subdues his anger only because of this kinship. See *BhP* X.89.4.

39. See also *PadmaP* VI.146.25, etc.

40. *Mbh* VIII.24.

41. *Mbh* VIII.24.127.

42. *Mbh* VIII.24.154–55.

43. See chapter 2. The Karṇaparvan account is further suspect on the grounds of a seeming contradiction growing out of Śiva's boon. If, as is made most explicit, Rāma is completely unskilled in the martial arts, why should Śiva choose him instead of a kṣatriya warrior to fight the demons? Further, if he conquers the mighty asuras when he is unarmed, what need has he for Śiva's divine weapons?

44. The purpose of the section in which this episode is found is to explain the transmission of the dhanurveda from Rāma to Karṇa, an event which, though paralleled in the case of other heroes of the Bhārata war, can hardly have belonged to the oldest Bhārgava tradition. See Sukthankar, "Bhṛgus and the Bhārata," p. 65.

45. *Mbh* III.186.81 ff.

46. *Mbh* XIV.52 ff.

47. See Sukthankar, "Bhṛgus and the Bhārata," pp. 48–49, 24–25.

48. The closest parallel to Cyavana's accomplishment is Viśvāmitra's bodily elevation of the cursed king Triśaṅku to the heavens in the face of the fierce opposition of Indra and the gods (*Rām.* I.59). Yet even Viśvāmitra, who appears to be capable of creating a whole new heaven in order to fulfill his vow, is ultimately induced to accept a compromise whereby his protégé is admitted to "heaven" upside down in the form of a new constellation that must, however, remain outside the path of the sun (ibid., v. 30–32). Before the wrath of Cyavana the gods must surrender unconditionally.

49. It is of interest here that the gods constitute Ṛcīka's wedding party.

50. See chapter 4 for further discussion of this connection.

51. It is the insufficiency of this reply which has, perhaps, impelled a southern interpolation to add a second explanation: "Thus indeed did the great sage become reknowned among the gods. He served as purohita of the daityas, too, in order to augment his glory." This was inserted after XII.278.32 by redactors of the MSS tradition represented by T2 (a Telugu MS) in the Crit. ed.

52. Yudhiṣṭhira's questions as to why Śukra destroyed the gods' splendor and how the hostility between the gods and demons arose go wholly unanswered.

53. Śukra is said to be the priest, counselor, and chaplain of generations of demon kings; his patrons are said to have included the demons Prahlāda (ŚA), Vṛṣaparvan (ŚK), and Bali (*BhP* VII.15 ff.).

54. These incidents accord well with Bhīṣma's statement at ŚŚ 7. This passage and, indeed, ŚA and ŚK as a whole are characterized by great emotionalism. See The asuras' tearful laments at ŚA 2–3 and 109–11, Śukra's anger at ŚA 102, and Devayānī's unrestrained suicidal grief over Kaca's deaths at ŚK 28–29, 37–38, and 45.

55. This is characteristic of Śukra in the purāṇic literature. Cf., for example, Śukra's curse of Prahlāda and the asuras at ŚA 102 with his curse of Bali at *BhP* VII.20.14–15, when the latter ignores his advice concerning the Vāmanāvatāra. In both stories, the curses are strangely otiose, bringing about only what had already been determined. Such overdetermination, however, is not uncommon in Indian myth.

Chapter 4. Masters of the Epic

1. The superimposition of the two pairs is hampered by the fact that in several myths, especially those of the Rāma complex, the themes of death are played out within the Bhṛguid group itself. This would be the case, for example, in the slaying of Reṇukā, where Bhārgava relations to other groups, gods, or kings are not involved.

2. In the Nahuṣa episode Cyavana wants to die and go to heaven with his beloved fish. The episode is reminiscent of the curious reference in the *ŚBr* to the Bhṛgus going to heaven en masse.

3. Examples are the secondary, and in some cases interpolated, episodes, Rāma and Śiva (*Mbh* VII.24), Rāma and Rāma Dāśarathi (*Mbh* Citr. ed. III.99.34 ff; Crit. ed. Āraṇyakaparvan app. I. no. 14; *Rām* I.73–75), Jamadagni and Sūrya (*Mbh* XIII.95), and Ṛcīka and Varuṇa (*Mbh* XIII.4).

4. The only connections to the kṣatriya subcycle are the debate between Devayānī and Śarmiṣṭhā over the relative status of kings and priests and the subsequent marriage of Devayānī to Yayāti, which ultimately involves the sage in a somewhat hostile encounter with the prince. The former instance is a stereotyped example of such a debate. It is notable, however, that the king in question is not a kṣatriya but the demon Vṛṣaparvan. The second, with its flavor of ksatriya love/hate, is especially interesting in that, like the stories of the descendants of Aurva, it connects Bhṛgus to the Yādavas, an important race of kṣatriyas.

5. The birth of Aurva as described at A 11 and that of Cyavana at *Mbh* I.6.3 are strikingly similar. Both are born prematurely at the time of violence directed against their mothers. Both are so brilliant at birth that they blind and destroy respectively the perpetrators of the violence. In both episodes it is asserted that the children derive their names from the unusual circumstances of their birth. Although unlike Aurva, the epic Cyavana is not said to have been ever the last surviving Bhārgava, this appears certainly to be the case in the *ŚBr* version of his central myth, where the Bhārgavas (or Āṅgirasas) depart for heaven as a group (*ŚBr* IV.1.5.1). In one case the sole survivor is a newborn child, in the other a senile man. See also chapter 3, note 57.

6. Thus, for example, the motif is very important in the various versions of the Śunaḥśepa myth and others involving Viśvāmitra (*ABr*. VII.18). It is interesting that in the *Rām*. account, which occurs as part of the *locus classicus* of

the Viśvāmitra cycle (*Rām* I.50–64), Sunaḥśepa, who is to become cherished as a son to Kauśika, is said to be the middle son of the Bhārgava Ṛcīka (*Rām* I.60.11–20).

7. See note 34 below.

8. *TS* 2.5.7, *JBr Upaniṣad* 2.8.1–6.

9. The anukramaṇikā names "Jamadagni or his son Rāma" as the ṛṣi of RV X.110; however, no mention is made of Rāma's career. The *ABr* (VII.27.3) has an obscure episode in which a figure called Rāma Mārgaveya gains admittance to the sacrifice for a group known as the Śyāparṇas. It has been suggested, because of the similarity of name, and perhaps because of the partial parallelism between the episode and that of Cyavana and the Aśvins, that Mārgaveya may be the prototype of the epic Rāma. However, the story is wholly lacking in elements of the career of the Bhārgava Rāma and I, therefore, am in agreement with Charpentier, who rejects this identification; see his "Paraśurāma," pp. 9–16.

10. Except for the similarity of ambivalence toward the gods, it is difficult to determine any clear affiliation between the two figures in the Veda. However, one interesting point arises from the fact that in the *RV* Cyavana is closely associated with the Aśvins, while Śukra is a friend, priest, and helper of Indra. This may have something to do with the apparent fusion of the Aśvins and Indra cults in the later epic Cyavana complex. Such a fusion might perhaps entail an association of originally unrelated priests like Cyavana and Śukra. This could be viewed as the first stage in the formation of what develops into the epic Bhārgava cycle.

11. See Hopkins, "Fountain of Youth," pp. 53–54.

12. Examples are: the second Bhārgava introduction to the epic ("Bhṛgus and the Bhārata," pp. 5–6); the interpolation of Bhārgava Rāma into the *ṣoda-Śarājakīya* or account of the sixteen kings (ibid., pp. 40–42); the introduction of Bhṛgu into the Nahuṣa story (ibid., pp. 55–56); and the second, Bhārgava-oriented opening to the epic itself (ibid., pp. 59–60).

13. The model here is undoubtedly Aurva. (See also reference to note 30, chapter 2.)

14. For an incisive summary and critique of some scholarly approaches to the problem, see "The Mahābhārata and its Critics," in Sukthankar's *On the Meaning of the Mahābhārata* (Bombay: Asiatic Society of Bombay, 1954), pp. 1–32.

15. That Rāma's slaughter accomplishes the goal of the Aurva-Rāma subcycle is confirmed by the fact that in this line Rāma has neither wife nor child. Having accomplished his purpose, he must retire from the world to avoid the contradiction inherent in his de facto rulership.

16. See Sukthankar, "Bhṛgus and the Bhārata," pp. 73–74.

17. For a list of these see note 15 to the Introduction. It is interesting to note that Bhārgava myth traces the ban on *surāpānam*, consumption of intoxicants, to Śukra's unfortunate experience. ŚK 54–55.

18. Such behavior contrasts strongly with the normative tradition of the epic itself. Thus, at *BhG* 3.35 Kṛṣṇa speaks for the tradition of mandatory ac-

ceptance of one's *svadharma*: "Better is one's own duty (*dharma*) imperfect than another's duty well done. Better is death in one's own duty; another's duty is dangerous."

19. The demon Mada (Intoxication) may be seen as another reference to Bhārgava association with unorthodox practices.

20. Karve, "Paraśurāma Myth," pp. 115–39.

21. F. Weller, "Who were the Bhṛguids?" ABORI 18 (1936–37), 297–98.

22. Charpentier, "Paraśurāma," pp. 9–16.

23. It is of great interest that this identification is stressed in the story of Vītahavya. The hostility between the Bhṛgus and the Vaitavyas is thus a real, although slender, link in the chain of the tradition. *AV* V.19.1.

24. Weller, "Who were the Bhṛguids?" pp. 279–99.

25. Charpentier, "Paraśurāma," p. 5.

26. *ŚBr* IV.1.2.10 ff. In another version, *JBr* II.128 ff, the sage Dadhyañc is introduced as the expounder of the head of the sacrifice. Unlike Cyavana he is hesitant for fear of Indra. He is induced to teach, however, after the resourceful Aśvins have replaced his head with that of a horse. When Indra cuts off the sage's horse-head, the Aśvins replace the original. At *BrahmāṇḍP* II.3.1.92 this sage is said to be a son of Cyavana and Sukanyā, although in the vedic literature he is generally reckoned as an Āṅgirasa or Ātharvana. See Hopkins, "The Fountain of Youth," pp. 50 ff.

27. *JBr* III.159–61. Interestingly, the *RV* identifies Uśanas Kāvya, or Śukra, as also being both protégé and helper of the Aśvins. *RV* I.117.12, VIII.23.17.

28. The *JBr* version also provides the origin of the Vaidanvat *sāmans*, the ritual chants, with which the Bhārgava Vidanvat successfully induced the frightened gods to return to the sacrifice.

29. The myth of Bhṛgu's curse of Agni, however, may perhaps be traced back to the *RV* description of the Bhṛgus as being the first to find fire and to bring it to men. (See note 9 to the Introduction.)

30. The Indic materials, from the Veda onward, support the idea of the gods and demons as parallel orders, each with its own king, priest, and sacrifices. See, for example, *ŚBr* XIII.4.3.

31. A complicating factor is the fact that in the *RV* the term *asura* is applied both to the demons and to many of the great gods. It is only later that the term becomes exclusively synonymous with *daitya* and *dānava*, the titanic foes of the gods. For a recent discussion of the asura-deva problem in Indo-Iranian studies, see T. Burrow, "The Proto Indoaryans," *JRAS* no. 2 (1973), pp. 126–40.

32. *ŚBr* IV.1.5.1 . . . *tac cyavano vā bhārgavaś cyavano vāṅgirasas* . . .

33. For a listing of these references and a discussion of their possible significance, see Maurice Bloomfield, *Hymns of the Atharva Veda*, Sacred Books of the East vol. 13 (New Delhi: Motilal Banarsidass, 1967), pp. xxvi–xxvii.

34. Śukra's participation in these deeds is recorded at *RV* IX.87.3, I.83.5. Cf. X.68.7, IV.50.5, II.23.18, where Bṛhaspati is lauded for the same acts. Śukra's association with Indra in the *RV* is extensive. He is helped by the god several times (*RV* X.99.9, VI.20.11) and aids him in destroying Śuṣṇa (*RV* I.51.10–11, V.29.9). The sage is even said to have fashioned the great vajra and presented it to Indra, feats usually associated with Tvaṣṭṛ (*RV* I.121.12, V.34.2; cf. *RV* I.32.2, V.31.4). On the basis of these references, Bergaigne identified Śukra with soma (*La religion védique*, II, 340). The identification seems improbable to me.

Bibliography

Primary Sources

Agnipurāṇa. Ānandāśrama Sanskrit Series, 41. Poona: Ānandāśrama Press, 1947.

Aitareya-Brāhmaṇa. Ānandāśrama Sanskrit Series, 32. Poona: Ānandāśrama Press, 1931.

Bhāgavatapurāṇa with Thirteen Commentaries, ed. by Kṛṣṇa Śaṅkar, Śāstrī. 10 vols. Kṛṣṇa Śaṅkar Śāstrī et al., Nadiyad, 1965.

Bhāvabhuti. *Mahāvīra-caritam*, ed. by Todar Mall. London: Oxford University Press, 1928.

Bhaviṣyapurāṇa. Bareli, 1969.

Brahmāṇḍapurāṇa, ed. by J. L. Shastri. Delhi: Motilal Banarsidass, 1973.

Brahmapurāṇa. Ānandāśrama Sanskrit Series, 28. Poona: Ānandāśrama Press, 1895.

Brahmavaivartapurāṇa. Ānandāśrama Sanskrit Series, 102. Poona: Ānandāśrama Press, 1935.

Jaiminīya-Brāhmaṇa, ed. by Vira-Chandra. Sarasvati-Vihara Series, vol. 31. Nagpur: International Academy of Indian Culture, 1954.

Liṅgapurāṇa. Bareli, 1969.

Mahābhārata: Critical Edition. ed, by V. S. Sukthankar, et al. 24 vols. (with Harivaṃśa and Pratīka Index). Poona: Bhandarkar Research Institute, 1933–70.

Mahābhārata, with Bhāratabhāvadīpa of Nīlakaṇṭha. 7 vols. (with Harivaṃśa). Poona: Citraśālā Press, 1930.

The Manusmṛti, with the commentary Manvarthamuktāvalī of Kullūka, ed. by N. R. Acharya. 10th ed. Bombay: Nirnaya Sāgar Press, 1946.

Matsyapurāṇa. Ānandāśrama Sanskrit Series, 54. Poona: Ānandāśrama Press, 1907.

Nāradapurāṇa, ed. by Hṛṣīkeśa Śāstri. Bib. Ind., 107. Calcutta: Asiatic Society of Bengal, 1891.

Nirukta of Yāska. Bombay Sanskrit and Prakrit Series, H. M. Bhandarkar, ed., no. 73. Bombay: Government Central Press, 1918.

Padmapurāṇa. Ānandāśrama Sanskrit Series, 131. Poona: Ānandāśrama Press, 1894.

Rāmāyaṇa of Vālmīki, with Three Commentaries, ed. by Mudholkar, Śrīnivāsa Śāstri. Bombay: Gujarati Printing Press, 1916.

Ṛgveda-Saṁhitā. 5 vols. Poona: Vaidikasaṃśodhana Maṇḍala, 1933–51.

Śatapatha-Brāhmaṇa, with Sāyana's Commentary. 5 vols. Bombay: Laxmi Venkateshwar Press, 1940.

Skandapurāṇa. Bombay: Veṅkateśvar Press, 1908.

Taittirīya-Āraṇyaka. Ānandāśrama Sanskrit Series, 6. Poona: Ānandāśrama Press, 1967.

Taittirīya-Saṃhitā. Ānandāśrama Sanskrit Series, 42. Poona: Ānandāśrama Press, 1961

Vālmīki-Rāmāyaṇa. Critical ed. by G. K. Bhatt, P. S. Vaidya, et al. Baroda: Oriental Institute of Baroda, 1960–75.

The Vāmanapurāṇa (with English trans.), ed. by S. Gupta. Varanasi: All-India Kashiraj Trust, 1968.

Vāyupurāṇa. 2 vols. Gurumandal Series, no. 19. Calcutta: Gurumandal Press, 1959.

Viṣṇudharmottarapurāṇa. Bombay: Veṅkateśvar Press, 1912.

Viṣṇupurāṇa. Bareli, 1967.

Secondary Sources

Achan, Anujan. "The Paraśurāma Legend and its Significance." Paper read at the eighth session of the All-India Oriental Conference, Mysore, 1935.

Aiyangar, Narayan. *Essays on Indo-Aryan Mythology*. Vol. 1, Bangalore: Caxton Press, 1898. Vol. 2, Madras: Addison, 1901.

Apte, V. S. *Practical Sanskrit-English Dictionary*. 3 vols. Poona: Prasad Prakashan, 1957.

Barth, A. *The Religions of India*. London: K. Paul, Trench, Trubner, 1901.

Belvalkar, S. K. *Uttararāmacarita of Bhavabhūti*. Harvard Oriental Series, vol. 21. Cambridge, Mass.: Harvard University Press, 1915.

Benveniste, E., and L. Renou. *Vṛta et Vṛthragna: étude de mythologie indo-iranienne.* Paris: Imprimerie Nationale, 1934.

Bergaigne, Abel. *La religion védique: d'après les hymnes du Ṛgveda.* 4 vols. 2d ed. Paris: Librairie Honoré Champion, 1963.

Bhandarkar, R. G. *Vaiṣnavism, Śaivism, and Minor Religious Systems.* Varanasi: Indological Book House, 1965.

Bhatt, G. H. *Pāda-Index of Vālmīki-Rāmāyaṇa.* Vol. 1. Gaekwad's Oriental Series, nos. 129, 153. Baroda: Oriental Institute, 1961.

Bhattacharji, S. *The Indian Theogony.* Cambridge: Cambridge University Press, 1970.

Biardeau, M. "La décapitation de Reṇukā dans le mythe de Paraśurāma," in *Pratidānam: Indian, Iranian and Indo-European Studies presented to T.B.J. Kuiper on his sixtieth birthday,* ed. by J. C. Heesterman et al. The Hague: Mouton, 1969.

Bloomfield, M. *The Atharva Veda.* Grundriss der Indo-Arischen Philologie und Alterthumskunde, vol. 2, book 1, pt. B. Strasbourg: Karl J. Trübner, 1899.

———. *Hymns of the Atharva Veda.* Sacred Books of the East, vol. 42. Delhi: Motilal Banarsidass, 1967.

———. "On the Art of Entering Another's Body: A Hindu Fiction Motif," *Proceedings of the American Philosophical Society,* 56 (1917), 1–44.

Brown, W. Norman. "The Basis of the Hindu Act of Truth," *Review of Religion,* 5 (1940), 36–45.

———. "The Creation Myth of the Ṛgveda," *JAOS,* 62, no. 2 (1942).

———. "Indra's Infancy According to Ṛgveda IV, 18," in *Dr. Siddheshwar Varma Presentation Volume.* Hoshiapur: Vishveshvaranand Vedic Research Institute, 1950.

———. "Proselytizing the Asuras (a note on Ṛgveda 10.124)," *JAOS,* 39, p. 1 (1919), 100–3.

Bunker, H. A. "Mother Murder in Myth and Legend," *Psychoanalytic Quarterly,* 13 (1944), 198–207.

Burlingame, E. W. "The Act of Truth (Saccākiriya): A Hindu Spell and its Employment as a Psychic Motif in Hindu Fiction," *JRAS,* 1917, pp. 429–67.

Caland, W. *Altindischer Ahnenkult.* Leiden: E. J. Brill, 1893.

Campbell, Joseph. *The Hero with a Thousand Faces.* New York: Meridian Books, 1956.

Carnoy, A. J., and A. B. Keith. *The Mythology of All Races*. Vol. 6, *Indo-Iranian Mythology*, ed. by S. H. Gray. Boston: Marshall Jones, 1917.

Charpentier, J. "Kleine Beiträge zur Indoiranischen Mythologie," *Uppsala Akademische Buchdruckerei*, 1911, pp. 1–24.

———. "Paraśurāma: The Main Outlines of his Legend," in *Kuppuswami Shastri Commemoration Volume*, pp. 9–16.

Chitrav, S. S. *Bhāratavarṣīya Prācīna Caritrakośa*. Poona: Bhāratīya Caritrakośa Mandal, 1964.

Cocchiara, G. *Il diavolo nella tradizione popolare italiana; paggi e recerche*. Palermo: G. B. Palumbo, 1945.

Conway, Moncure Daniel. *Demonology and Devil Lore*. New York: Henry Holt, 1881.

Cox, George W. *The Mythology of the Aryan Nations*. 2 vols. London: Longmans, Green, 1870.

———. *Things Indian*. London: J. Murray, 1906.

Crooke, W. *Popular Religion and Folklore of Northern India*. 2 vols. Westminster: Constable, 1896.

Dalton, E. T. *Descriptive Ethnology of Bengal*. Calcutta: K. S. Mukhopadhyaya, 1960.

Dange, S. A. "Death and Rebirth in Initiation Ceremonies," *Indian Antiquary*, 3d ser., 1, no. 2 (1964).

———. "Field and the 'Ritual-Husband' (from the Vedic Tradition," *JUN*, 19, pts. 1 and 2 (1968), 1–28.

———. *Legends in the Mahābhārata*. Delhi and Varanasi: Motilal Banarsidass, 1969.

———. "Virgin and the Divine Seed-Layer, (Rg.V. X.61)," *JIH*, 24, pt. 2, 134 (1967), 369–98.

Deva, Raja Radhakanta. *Śabdakalpadruma*. 3d ed. 5 vols. Varaṇasi: Chowkhambha Sanskrit Series Office, 1967.

Devasthali, G. V. *Religion and Mythology of the Brāhmaṇas*. Bhau Vishnu Ashtekar Vedic Research Series, 1. Poona: Poona University Press, 1956.

Dikshitar, V. R. R. *The Purāṇa Index*. Madras: University of Madras, 1955.

Dixit, G. P. "A Textual Comparison of the Story of Yayāti as found in the Mahābhārata and the Matsya-purāṇa," in *Proceedings of the Fifth Indian Oriental Conference*, Lahore, 1930. Vol. 1, pp. 721 ff.

Dowson, John. *A Classical Dicitonary of Hindu Mythology*. London: Routledge and Kegan Paul, 1961.

Dubois, J. N. *Hindu Manners, Customs and Ceremonies*, trans. from the French by H. K. Beauchamp. 3d ed. Oxford: Clarendon Press, 1936.

Eliade, M. *Myth and Reality*. New York: Harper and Row, 1963.

———. *Rites and Symbols of Initiation*. New York: Harper and Row, 1963.

Elmore, W. T. *Dravidian Gods in Modern Hinduism: A Study of the Local and Village Deities of Southern India*. University Studies Series, vol. 15, no. 1. Lincoln, Neb.: University of Nebraska, 1915.

Fergusson, J. *Tree and Serpent Worship*. 2d. ed. London: India Museum, W. H. Allen, 1915.

Filliozat, Jean. *Étude de démonologie indienne: le Kumāra-tantra de Rāvaṇa et les textes paralleles tibétains, chinois, cambogiens, et arabes*. Cahier de la Societé Asiatique, no. 4. Paris: Societé Asiatique, 1937.

Freud, Sigmund. *Totem and Taboo*. London: Routledge and Kegan Paul, 1960.

Frye, Northrop. "New Directions from Old," in *Myth and Mythmaking*, ed. by H. Murray. Boston: Beacon Press, 1960.

Garcon, Maurice, and Jean Vendron. *The Devil: An Historical, Critical, and Medical Study*, trans. by S. H. Guest. New York: E. P. Dutton, 1930.

Goldman, R. "Akṛtavraṇa vs. Śrīkṛṣṇa as Narrators of the Legend of Bhārgava Rāma *à propos* Some Observations of Dr. V. S. Sukthankar," *ABORI*, 53 (1970), 161–73.

———. "Mortal Man and Immortal Woman: A New Interpretation of Three Ākhyāna Hymns of the Rgveda," *JOIB*, 18, no. 4 (1969), 273–303.

———. "Myth and Literature: A Translation of Matsya Purāṇa 47," *Mahfil*, 7, (1971), 45–62.

———. "Some Observations on the Paraśu of Paraśurāma," *JOIB*, 21, no. 3 (1972), 153–65.

———. Vālmīki and the Bhṛgu Connection," *JAOS*, 96, no. 1 (1976), 97–101.

———, and J. L. Mason. "Who Knows Rāvaṇa: A Narrative Difficulty in the Vālmīki Rāmāyaṇa," *ABORI*, 50 (1969), 95–100.

Gore, N. A. *A Bibliography of the Rāmāyaṇa*. Poona: Pub. by the author, 1943.

Hastings, J., ed. *Encyclopedia of Religion and Ethics*. Edinburgh: T. T. Clark, 1959.

Henry, V. "Dadhikrā-Dadhikrāvan et l'euhemerisme en exégèse védique," in *Album Kern*. Leiden, 1903. Pp. 5–12.

Henry, Victor. *La Magie dans l'Inde Antique*. Paris: Dujarrie, 1904.

Heras, Rev. H. S. J. "The Devil in Indian Scripture," *Journal of the Bombay Branch of the Royal Asiatic Society*, 27, pt. 2 (June 1952), 214–41.

Hillebrandt, Alfred. *Vedische Mythologie*. 2 vols. Hildesheim: Georg Olms Verlagsbuchhandlung, 1965.

The Holy Lake of the Acts of Rama, trans. by W. D. Hill. Trans. of Tulasī Dās's *Rāmacaritamānasa*. London: Oxford University Press, 1952.

Hopkins, E. Washburn. "Allusions to the Rāmāyaṇa in the Mahābhārata," *JAOS*, 50 (1930), 85–103.

———. *Epic Mythology*. Strasbourg: Karl J. Trübner, 1915.

———. "The Fountain of Youth," *JAOS*, 26, pt. 1 (1905).

———. *The Great Epic of India*. Calcutta: Punthi Pustak, 1969.

———. "Magic Observances in the Hindu Epic," *Proceedings of the American Philosophical Society*, 49 (1910), 20–43.

———. *The Mutual Relations of the Four Castes According to the Mānavadharmaśāstram*. Leipzig: Breitkopf and Hartel, 1881.

———. "The Oath in the Hindu Epic," *JAOS*, 52 (1932), 316–33.

———. "The Original Rāmāyaṇa," *JAOS*, 46 (1926), 202–19.

———. "Proverbs and Tales Common to the Two Sanskrit Epics," *AJP*, 20, no. 77 (1899), 22–40.

———. *The Religions of India*. Boston and London: Ginn, 1895.

Hymns of the Atharva-Veda, trans. by Maurice Bloomfield. Sacred Books of the East, vol. 42. Reprint. Delhi: Motilal Banarasidass, 1964.

Jacobi, Hermann. *The Rāmāyaṇa*, trans. by S. N. Ghosal. Baroda: Oriental Institute of Baroda, 1960.

Janaki, S. S. 'Paraśurāma," *Puranam*, 7, no. 1 (1966), 52–82.

Kantawala, S. G. *Cultural History from the Matsyapurāṇa*. Baroda: The Maharaja Sayajirao University, 1964.

———. "Geographical and Ethnic Data in the Matsya Purāṇa," *Puranam*, 5, no. 1 (1963).

Karmarkar, A. P. "Dr. V. S. Sukthankar's Theory of the Bhṛguization of the Original Bhārata and the Light It Throws on the Dravidian Problem," *ABORI*, 20 (1938–3), 19–26.

Karve, I. "The Paraśurāma Myth," *JUB*, 1 (1932), 115–39.

Keith, A. B. *The Religion and Philosophy of the Veda and Upaniṣads*. Cambridge, Mass.: Harvard University Press, 1925.

———. *The Veda of the Black Yajus School (entitled Taittirīya Saṃhitā)*. Harvard Oriental Series, vol. 19. Reprint, 2 vols. Delhi and Varanasi: Motilal Banarsidass, 1967.

———, and A. A. MacDonell. *Vedic Index of Names and Subjects*. Reprint. Varanasi: Motilal Banarsidass, 1958.

Kosambi, D. D. *Introduction to the Study of Indian History*. Bombay: Popular Book Depot, 1956.

———. *Myth and Reality*. Bombay: Popular Prakashan, 1962.

Kuhn, A. "Die Herabkunft des Feuers und des Göttertranks," in *Mythologische Studien*. Guterslok: C. Bertelsman, 1886.

Kurulkar, G. M. "Demons of Hindu Mythology with Special Reference to their Body Forms," *Journal of the Anthropological Society of Bombay*, n.s. 1, no. 1 (1946), 81–110.

Lassen, Christian. *Indische Alterthumskunde*. 2d ed. Vol. 1. Leipzig: L. A. Kittler, 1867.

Lévi-Strauss, Claude. *The Raw and the Cooked*, trans. by J. and D. Weightman. New York: Harper and Row, 1969.

———. "The Structural Study of Myth," in *Myth: A Symposium*, ed. by Thomas A. Sebeok. Bloomington: Indiana University Press, 1955.

MacDonell, A. A. "Mythological Studies in Ṛgveda," *JRAS*, 1895, pp. 168–77.

———. Vedic Mythology. Grundriss der Indo-Arischen Philologie und Altertumskunde von G. Buhler, vol. 1, book 1, pt. A. Strasbourg: Karl J. Trübner, 1897.

MacDonell, A. A. *The Vedic Mythology*. Varanasi: Indological Book House, 1963.

Majumdar, R. C., ed. *The History and Culture of the Indian People*. 11 vols. 4th ed. Bombay: Bharatiya Vidya Bhavan, 1968.

Masson, J. L. and M. V. Patwardhan. *Śāntarasa and Abhinavagupta's Philosophy of Aesthetics*. Poona: Bhandarkar Oriental Research Institute, 1969.

Monier-Williams, M. *Brahmanism and Hinduism*. New York: Macmillan, 1891.

Monro, W. D. *Stories of Indian Gods and Heroes*. London: George G. Harrap, 1912.

Muir, J. "Manu, a Progenitor of Aryan India," *JRAS*, 20 (1888), 410–16.

———. "On the Relation of Priests to the Other Classes of Society in the Vedic Age," *JRAS*, 1866.

———. *Original Sanskrit Texts.* 5 vols. 2d ed. Amsterdam: Oriental Press, 1967.

Munshi, K. M., and R. R. Diwakar, eds. *Studies in Epic and Purāṇas of India.* Bombay: Bharatiya Vidya Bhavan, 1963.

Murray, Henry A., ed. *Myth and Mythmaking.* Boston: Beacon Press, 1968.

Narasimhacar, S. S. "The Jain Rāmāyaṇas," *IHQ*, 15 (1939), 574–95.

The Ocean of Story, trans. by C. H. Tawney, ed. by N. M. Penzer. Trans. of Somadeva's *Kathāsaritsāgara.* 10 vols. London: Chas. Sawyer, 1942.

O'Flaherty, Wendy D. *Asceticism and Eroticism in the Mythology of Śiva.* Oxford: Oxford University Press, 1973.

———. *Hindu Myths.* Middlesex: Penguin, 1975.

———. "The Submarine Mare in the Mythology of Śiva," *JRAS*, no. 1 (1971), 9–27.

Oldenberg, H. "Ākhyāna-Hymnen in Ṛgveda," *ZDMG*, 29 (1885), 52–90.

———. *Die Religion des Veda.* Stuttgart and Berlin: J. G. Cotta, 1917.

Oppert, Gustav. *The Original Inhabitants of India.* Westminister: Constable, 1863.

Pañcaviṁśa-Brāhmaṇa, trans. by Caland. Calcutta: Asiatic Society of Bengal, 1931.

Pargiter, F., ed. *The Purāṇa, Text of the Dynasties of the Kali Age.* Chowkhamba Sanskrit Series, 5. Varanasi: Chowkamba Sanskrit Series Office, 1962.

Perry, E. D. "Indra in the Ṛg Veda," *JAOS*, 2, pp. 199–205.

Przyluski, J. V. "Epic Studies," *IHQ*, 15 (1939), 289–99.

Pusalker, A. D. "Literary and Archeological Evidence on the Aryan Expansion in India," *Puranam*, 6, no. 2 (1964), 307–32.

Raglan, Lord. *The Hero: A Study in Tradition, Myth and Drama.* New York: Vintage Books, 1956.

Ramdas, G. "Rāvaṇa and His Tribes," *IHQ*, 5 (1929), 281–99; 6 (1930), 285–89.

Rank, Otto. *The Myth of the Birth of the Hero*, trans. by T. Robbins and S. E. Jelliffe. New York: Robert Brunner, 1952.

Roth, R. "Brahma und die Brähmanen, *ZDMG*, 1 (1847), 66 ff.

———. "Die höchsten Götter der arischen Völker," *ZDMG*, 6 (1852), 67–68.

———. *Zur Literature und Geschichte des Veda*. Stuttgart: A. Leisching, 1846.

Roy. S. M. "On the Date of the Brahmāṇḍapūraṇa," *Puranam*, 5, no. 2 (1963), 305–19.

The Śatapatha-Brāhmaṇa, trans. by J. Eggeling. 5 vols. Sacred Books of the East, vols. 12, 26, 41, 43, 44. Reprint. Delhi: Motilal Banarsidass, 1963.

Sebeok, Thomas A., ed. *Myth: A Symposium*. Bloomington and London: Indiana University Press, 1955.

Sen, (Rai Sahib) Dineshchandra. *The Bengali Rāmāyaṇa*. Calcutta: University of Calcutta Press, 1920.

Sen, N. M. "Some Linguistic Aberrations in the Matsya-purāṇa," *Puranam*, 5, no. 2 (1963), 346–49.

Shende, N. J. "The Authorship of the Mahābhārata," *ABORI*, 24, pp. 81 ff.

Singer, Milton, ed. *Kṛṣṇa: Myths, Rites and Attitudes*. Chicago: University of Chicago Press. 1968.

The Śiva-Purāṇa. Ancient Indian Tradition and Mythology Series, vols. 1 and 2. Varanasi: Motilal Banarsidass, 1970.

Sorensen, S. *An Index to the Names in the Mahābhārata*. New Delhi: Motilal Banarsidass, 1963.

Sukthankar, V. S. *Analecta*. Sukthankar Memorial Edition, vol. 2, ed. by P. K. Gode. Bombay: Karnatak Publishing House, 1945.

———. "The Bhṛgus and the Bhārata: A Text-Historical Study," *ABORI*, 18, pp. 1–76.

———. *Critical Studies in the Mahābhārata*. Sukthankar Memorial Edition, vol. 1, ed. by P. K. Gode. Bombay: Karnatak Publishing House, 1944.

———. *On the Meaning of the Mahābhārata*. Bombay: The Asiatic Society of Bombay, 1954.

Thomas, F. W. "Tibetan Versions of the Rāmāyaṇa," *Indian Studies*, Laumann Memorial Volume, pp. 193–212.

Van Buitenen, J. A. B. *The Mahābhārata.* Vols. 1–2. Chicago: University of Chicago Press, 1974–75.

The Vishnu Purāṇa, trans. by H. H. Wilson. 3d ed. Calcutta: Punthi Pustak, 1961.

Vogel, J. P. *Indian Serpent Lore.* London: Arthur Probsthain, 1926.

Walhouse, M. J. "The Belief in Bhutas: Devil and Ghost Worship in Western India," *Journal of the Anthropological Institute*, 5 (1876), 408–23.

Wheeler, J. Talboys. *History of India from the Earliest Times.* Vol. 3. London: Karl J. Trübner, 1874.

Weber. A. "A Jain Legend of Rāvaṇa from the Śatruñjayamahātmya," *Indian Antiquary*, 30 (1901), 289–351.

———. "Rāmāyaṇa," *Indian Antiquary*, 4 (1875), 247–49.

Weller, F. "Who Were the Bhṛguids?" *ABORI*, 18 (1936–37), 297 ff.

Wilkins, W. J. *Hindu Mythology.* Calcutta: Thacker, Spink, 1882.

Winternitz, M. *A History of Indian Literature.* Vol. 1. Trans. by S. Ketkar. Calcutta: University of Calcutta Press, 1927–33.

Ziegenbalg, B. *Gods of Malabar.* Madras: Selbstverlag des Herausgebers, 1867.

Zimmer, H. *Maya, Der Indische Mythos.* Stuttgart, 1936.

*Index**

* I should like to express here my thanks to Mr. James George Ebin of the University of California for his assistance in the preparation of this index.

Studies in Oriental Culture

1. *The Ōnin War: History of Its Origins and Background, with a Selective Translation of the Chronicle of Ōnin*, by H. Paul Varley 1967
2. *Chinese Government in Ming Times: Seven Studies*, ed. Charles O. Hucker 1969
3. *The Actors' Analects* (*Yakusha Rongo*), ed. and tr. by Charles J. Dunn and Bunzō Torigoe 1969
4. *Self and Society in Ming Thought*, by Wm. Theodore de Bary and the Conference on Ming Thought. Also in paperback ed. 1970
5. *A History of Islamic Philosophy*, by Majid Fakhry 1970
6. *Phantasies of a Love Thief: The Caurapañcāśikā Attributed to Bilhaṇa*, by Barbara Stoler Miller 1971
7. *Iqbal: Poet-Philosopher of Pakistan*, ed. Hafeez Malik 1971
8. *The Golden Tradition: An Anthology of Urdu Poetry*, by Ahmed Ali. Also in paperback ed. 1973
9. *Conquerors and Confucians: Aspects of Political Change in Late Yüan China*, by John W. Dardess 1973
10. *The Unfolding of Neo-Confucianism*, by Wm. Theodore de Bary and the Conference on Seventeenth-Century Chinese Thought. Also in paperback ed. 1975
11. *To Acquire Wisdom: The Way of Wang Yang-ming*, by Julia Ching 1976

12. *Gods, Priests, and Warriors: The Bhṛgus of the Mahābhārata*, by Robert P. Goldman 1977
13. *Mei Yao-ch'en and the Development of Early Sung Poetry*, by Jonathan Chaves 1976

Translations from the Oriental Classics

Major Plays of Chikamatsu, tr. Donald Keene 1961

Four Major Plays of Chikamatsu, tr. Donald Keene. Paperback text edition. 1961

Records of the Grand Historian of China, translated from the Shih chi of Ssu-ma Ch'ien, tr. Burton Watson, 2 vols. 1961

Instructions for Practical Living and Other Neo-Confucian Writings by Wang Yang-ming, tr. Wing-tsit Chan 1963

Chuang Tzu: Basic Writings, tr. Burton Watson, paperback ed. only 1964

The Mahābhārata, tr. Chakravarthi V. Narasimhan. Also in paperback ed. 1965

The Manyōshū, Nippon Gakujutsu Shinkōkai edition 1965

Su Tung-p'o: Selections from a Sung Dynasty Poet, tr. Burton Watson 1965

Bhartrihari: Poems, tr. Barbara Stoler Miller. Also in paperback ed. 1967

Basic Writings of Mo Tzu, Hsün Tzu, and Han Fei Tzu, tr. Burton Watson. Also in separate paperback eds. 1967

The Awakening of Faith, Attributed to Aśvaghosha, tr. Yoshito S. Hakeda. Also in paperback ed. 1967

Reflections on Things at Hand: The Neo-Confucian Anthology, comp. Chu Hsi and Lü Tsu-ch'ien, tr. Wing-tsit Chan 1967

The Platform Sutra of the Sixth Patriarch, tr. Philip B. Yampolsky 1967

Essays in Idleness: The Tsurezuregusa of Kenkō, tr. Donald Keene. Also in paperback ed. 1967

The Pillow Book of Sei Shōnagon, tr. Ivan Morris, 2 vols. 1967

Two Plays of Ancient India: The Little Clay Cart and the Minister's Seal, tr. J. A. B. van Buitenen 1968

The Complete Works of Chuang Tzu, tr. Burton Watson 1968

The Romance of the Western Chamber (*Hsi Hsiang chi*) tr. S. I. Hsiung. Also in paperback ed. 1968

The Manyōshū, Nippon Gakujutsu Shinkōkai edition. Paperback text edition. 1969

Records of the Historian: Chapters from the Shih chi of Ssu-ma Ch'ien. Paperback text edition, tr. Burton Watson 1969

Cold Mountain: 100 Poems by the T'ang Poet Han-shan, tr. Burton Watson. Also in paperback ed. 1970

Twenty Plays of the Nō Theatre, ed. Donald Keene. Also in paperback ed. 1970

Chūshingura: The Treasury of Loyal Retainers, tr. Donald Keene. Also in paperback ed. 1971

The Zen Master Hakuin: Selected Writings, tr. Philip B. Yampolsky 1971

Chinese Rhyme-Prose: Poems in the Fu Form from the Han and Six Dynasties Periods, tr. Burton Watson. Also in paperback ed. 1971

Kūkai: Major Works, tr. Yoshito S. Hakeda 1972

The Old Man Who Does as He Pleases: Selections from the Poetry and Prose of Lu Yu, tr. Burton Watson 1973

The Lion's Roar of Queen Śrīmālā, tr. Alex & Hideko Wayman 1974

Courtier and Commoner in Ancient China: Selections from the History of The Former Han by Pan Ku, tr. Burton Watson 1974

Japanese Literature in Chinese. Vol. I: Poetry and Prose in Chinese by Japanese Writers of the Early Period, tr. Burton Watson 1975

Japanese Literature in Chinese. Vol. II: Poetry and Prose in Chinese by Japanese Writers of the Later Period, tr. Burton Watson 1976

Scripture of the Lotus Blossom of the Fine Dharma, tr. Leon Hurvitz. Also in paperback ed. 1976

Love Song of the Dark Lord: Jayadeva's Gītagovinda, tr. Barbara Stoler Miller. Also in paperback ed. Cloth ed. includes critical text of the Sanskrit. 1977

Companions to Asian Studies

Approaches to the Oriental Classics, ed. Wm. Theodore de Bary 1959

Early Chinese Literature, by Burton Watson. Also in paperback ed. 1962

Approaches to Asian Civilization, ed. Wm. Theodore de Bary and Ainslie T. Embree 1964

The Classic Chinese Novel: A Critical Introduction, by C. T. Hsia. Also in paperback ed. 1968

Chinese Lyricism: Shih Poetry from the Second to the Twelfth Century, tr. Burton Watson. Also in paperback ed. 1971

A Syllabus of Indian Civilization, by Leonard A. Gordon and Barbara Stoler Miller 1971

Twentieth-Century Chinese Stories, ed. C. T. Hsia and Joseph S. M. Lau. Also in paperback ed. 1971

A Syllabus of Chinese Civilization, by J. Mason Gentzler, 2d ed. 1972

A Syllabus of Japanese Civilization, by H. Paul Varley, 2d ed. 1972

An Introduction to Chinese Civilization, ed. John Meskill, with the assistance of J. Mason Gentzler 1973

An Introduction of Japanese Civilization, ed. Arthur E. Tiedemann 1974

A Guide to Oriental Classics, ed. Wm. Theodore de Bary and Ainslie T. Embree, 2d ed. Also in paperback ed. 1975

Introduction to Oriental Civilizations

Wm. Theodore de Bary, *Editor*

Sources of Japanese Tradition	1958	Paperback ed., 2 vols.	1964
Sources of Indian Tradition	1958	Paperback ed., 2 vols.	1964
Sources of Chinese Tradition	1960	Paperback ed., 2 vols.	1964